Philosophy and the Modern African American Freedom Struggle

THE BLACK ATLANTIC CULTURAL SERIES: REVISIONING
ARTISTIC, HISTORICAL, LITERARY, PSYCHOLOGICAL,
AND SOCIOLOGICAL PERSPECTIVES

Series Editor: Emily Allen-Williams, Director, Educational Research Analysis & Consultation, LLC

This series will embrace exploratory discussions that emanate from the latest Africana ideas from the Caribbean, Black Atlantic, and Southern United States. The series aims to examine ideologies, theories, aesthetics, and their cultural and global manifestations. From the music, dance, literature, fashion, linguistic nuances, and beyond, Africana culture is vibrantly original and requires significant documentation to avoid its loss in the vast imitation that abounds nationally and internationally.

RECENT TITLES IN THE SERIES:

Art and Ritual in the Black Diaspora: Archetypes of Transition, by Paul A. Griffith

Recovering the African Feminine Divine in Literature, the Arts, and Practice: Yemonja Awakening, edited by LaJuan Simpson-Wilkey, Sheila Smith McKoy, and Eric Bridges

Philosophy and the Modern African American Freedom Struggle: A Freedom Gaze, by Anthony Sean Neal

Philosophy and the Modern African American Freedom Struggle

A Freedom Gaze

Anthony Sean Neal
Foreword by Leonard Harris

LEXINGTON BOOKS
Lanham • Boulder • New York • London

Published by Lexington Books
An imprint of The Rowman & Littlefield Publishing Group, Inc.
4501 Forbes Boulevard, Suite 200, Lanham, Maryland 20706
www.rowman.com

6 Tinworth Street, London SE11 5AL, United Kingdom

Copyright © 2022 The Rowman & Littlefield Publishing Group, Inc.

All rights reserved. No part of this book may be reproduced in any form or by any electronic or mechanical means, including information storage and retrieval systems, without written permission from the publisher, except by a reviewer who may quote passages in a review.

British Library Cataloguing in Publication Information Available

Library of Congress Cataloging-in-Publication Data Available

ISBN 978-1-7936-4051-2 (cloth)
ISBN 978-1-7936-4052-9 (electronic)
ISBN 978-1-7936-4053-6 (pbk.)

Contents

Foreword   vii
    By Leonard Harris

Preface   ix

Acknowledgments   xiii

Chapter 1: Struggling for Freedom Between Death (Slavery) and Life   1

Chapter 2: The New Negro's Negritude   21

Chapter 3: From Harlem to Paris (And Back)   47

Chapter 4: From Montgomery to West Africa   67

Chapter 5: From Freedom to Fragmentation through Liberalism   89

Bibliography   103

Index   107

About the Author   115

Foreword

By Leonard Harris

It is courageous to face irredeemable loss in this life, address its moral meaning and yet proffer indominable hope. It is magnanimous to confront competing concepts of identity, consider the valuable contributions of each, even if enigmatic, without succumbing to crass condemnation of indefensible conceptions.

Without "Life," nothing follows. The precondition for a phenomenology of consciousness is the existence of its embodied corporeal "Life" in all its complexity. We see the role of "Life" in *Philosophy and the African American Modern Freedom Struggle: A Freedom Gaze*; we see how the "freedom gaze" has constituted competing forms of consciousness; we see the role of "Freedom" intrinsic to the being of "Life" despite controversy and are able to see because of a different reading of African American history—a reading of African American history that begins from facing the problem of evil—a good God that allows the evil of racial slavery—to the problem of the modern era's internal racial class divide—upper-class African Americans separated from a lower-class population with little to no opportunities. Weaving both the secular and the sacred, from *Why, Lord?* (Anthony B. Pinn) to *The Jesse Jackson Phenomenon: The Purpose in Afro-American Politics* (Adolph Reed), the way common culture itself weaves both the secular and the sacred into a tapestry of being, results in foregrounding issues often left unspoken or unseen.

Philosophy and the African American Modern Freedom Struggle: A Freedom Gaze argues for and finds common ground in African American pursuits of freedom, minimally, the ability to pursue goals without the wretched humiliation and loss caused by racial discrimination. It argues for common ground while treading the often-uneasy accommodations between humanitarian values of freedom as liberty and sacred values that require faith even against popular liberties. There have been, for example, radically different concepts of what it is to be black and what the phenomenology of its experience demands, whether the *Black Atlantic* multi-variations of race or a Black Nationalist essentialist definition of race and its singular genuine experience. *Philosophy and the African American Modern Freedom Struggle: A Freedom Gaze*, however, offers a picture of the Black experience as a river of experiments, responses, and variations on a common theme of "Freedom."

Rooted in venerable African American traditions, the text simultaneously stands away from those traditions to shine a light in a new direction as *a philosophy born of struggle*—it is no longer a repetition of the same but a voice that comes into its own by its own weaving. Consequently, this Foreword is a prolegomenon to what has yet to be sufficiently heard because it stands on philosophical grounds that are new to minds, offering a way to see African American life as itself a making of a gaze. Seeing the object can only come after the kind of critical reflection the author argues is needed.

Arguably, *Philosophy and the African American Modern Freedom Struggle: A Freedom Gaze*, will face challenges to its descriptive claim that the freedom gaze is an integral, if unnamed, feature of the Black experience. It may be challenged and queried regarding whether the crucial role of religion is a bane, crutch, or sustaining source of effective agency. Is the "Black experience" a misnomer, given the historic class divide, rendering substantively different experiences without a central core or common quest? And it will face challenges to its philosophic approach of treating the Black experience as a phenomenology with a telos of freedom. The controversies will stand on a platform created by a new weaving and thereby invariably continue the river within which the *Philosophy and the African American Modern Freedom Struggle: A Freedom Gaze* flows.

Preface

Freedom, as a general goal and antecedent for the development of culture, the instigation of behavior, and the creation of a black phenomenology, is the name given to a movement. It is the goal of this work to describe the ideas that defined one of the movement's subdivisions, which will be referred to as the *Modern Era*. The modern era of the *Freedom Movement* ideologically developed from a theory which I have employed to conceptualize the placement of ideas, a dialectical method which creates the ability to discuss the overall freedom movement, by diaspora Africans in the Americas as divisible into certain moments within the freedom movement, containing not only specific goals, but also sharing in the general goal of freedom. These concepts were alluded to in my earlier publication, *Common Ground: A Comparison of the Ideas of Consciousness in the Writings of Howard W. Thurman and Huey P. Newton* (Africa World Press, 2015); however, the description was abridged. Describing the idea of the modern era of the freedom movement in this book in terms of this subdivision serves the purpose of depicting how a philosophy of freedom was infused into the common culture. It also demonstrates the transference of ideas and defines the overall intellectual intentionality of the moment.

This work can be categorized as philosophy, fitting neatly into three subcategories: historical philosophy, descriptive aesthetics, and phenomenology. From the historical perspective, this work will engage questions such as how the historical experience of oppression and the denial of humanity created space for the development of a certain consciousness and ideas about how to create intentional shifts in consciousness. The existence and demonstration of agency within the ideas of the diaspora African and the creation of an intentional community with the aim of defining and attaining freedom will also be dissected with the purpose of understanding the black community (as a whole) in the modern era. Additionally, the ability of these ideas to address times beyond the modern era, inclusive of the present, will be analyzed.

Several core themes will be probed in order to bring clarity to this topic. Among these themes are experience, knowledge, consciousness, unity, community development/social transformation, and freedom. These themes will be used to form the conceptual framework of this manuscript. Other themes that will be prominent are Du Boisianism, Harlem Renaissance, Africana Canon, Black Atlantic, blackness, diaspora, African Freedom Aesthetic, self-definition, and revolution.

The basic argument of this work begins post-consideration of the effect that the experience of violent oppression and anti-Black racism had on people of African descent in the Americas (and other locations), and argues that this effect created the conscious desire for freedom which, although the desire was not singularly defined or expressed, became a pronounced part of the culture such that it was the impetus for a social movement known, henceforth, as the *Freedom Movement*. The Freedom Movement had many leaders with differing strategies; however, their desired aim was the same. Those involved recognized this aim as freedom. If a social movement is defined as a prolonged action or actions by a group or groups with the aim of some social or political change, then the Freedom Movement waged by people of African descent in the Americas, with its contacts around the world, is one of the *most significant movements* known to the Americas.

The goal of this study both separates it and gives it uniqueness. With this book, I seek to create a useful basis for the identification of common lines of thought in the writings of Africana social thinkers from the modern era. Identification of common lines such as these are useful in the analysis of memes and the demonstration of the ability of oppression to create a separate perceptual framework which gives rise to vastly different conceptions of nations and even worlds. Groundwork is also developed for the creation of a black canon of phenomenological thought, thus giving space within which to situate the works of Africana social thinkers of the modern era, especially those who created philosophies of community development/social transformation based squarely on the experience of blackness. Blackness (or the Black experience in America) will be shown to be a major determinant in the creation of a cultural consciousness aimed at defining and attaining freedom in the modern era.

Several years ago when I was completing my dissertation, I uncovered many of the themes previously mentioned. Specifically, the theme of the modern era, which was central in framing my ideas and providing a context from which to juxtapose my perceptual framework in an effort to work toward creating a phenomenological description of the African freedom movement within the modern era. While my educational research has the requisite depth, it also has a deep level of interdisciplinary training which allows for a multifaceted perspective on this this particular book topic. Previously, I have published in the areas of political philosophy, historical philosophy, religion, and African American Studies while maintaining a current open lines of communication with members in *Philosophy Born of Struggle*, a professional organization of black philosophers.

My first book was *Common Ground: A Comparison of the Ideas of Consciousness in the Writings of Howard W. Thurman and Huey P. Newton* (Africa World Press, 2015). In this work, the subject of raising community consciousness as a means of community development and social transformation was explored. While studying this concept, the period of 1896 to1975 was focused upon as the years that shaped the modern era of the African American freedom struggle. It was during this period that the first cadre of academically trained African American scholars, who dedicated the bulk of their scholarship toward the goal of African American social transformation, came into prominence. I wrote an article—"Connecting the Ideological Lineage: From W. E. B. Du Bois to Huey P. Newton"—detailing this trend. published in the *Journal of Pan African Studies* (2016/7).

My second book, *Love Against Fragmentation: Howard Thurman's Philosophical Mysticism* (Lexington Books, 2019) demonstrates how African American philosophy and African American philosophers have played a central role in understanding and shaping what it means to be black in America. Yet, with the mass exodus of black students from HBCUs after the Civil Rights Era, many of the important figures and their inquiries have been (notably) seldom or poorly studied. My aim in this book was to grapple with one seminal figure, his memory of his ancestors, and the education he received from Morehouse College (Atlanta University Center), all of which formed the roots of the ideologies he later produced.

Howard Thurman's deep-rooted knowledge of black culture, particularly black religious ideas as they existed during the period of African enslavement in the United States and as they are exhibited in the Negro spirituals, shaped his thinking and allowed him to produce a body of work grounded in the musings and traditions of his ancestors. Throughout this book, I investigated, formed an analysis, and critiqued Thurman's work such that others can benefit from the profundity of his thoughts while also taking note of their relevance for today's philosophers concerned with humanity. In terms of my current published work and thoughts as I have made my way to this current research, I continue to focus on political philosophy, philosophy of religion, and aesthetics. I regard these areas as important in my struggle to gain clarity concerning the Black experience through the use of philosophy. I take this struggle to have a humanistically existential focus on understanding personhood, human rights, and human potential.[1]

NOTE

1. In the year 1896, a line in the sand for the modern era of the African American freedom movement, a shift in the legal status of blacks in America occurred, predicated by the decision in the *Plessy v. Ferguson* Supreme Court trial. By coincidence, it was also the year in which the publication of W. E. B. Du Bois's dissertation, from Harvard occurred. With this publication began an era of formally trained black scholars studying the black condition and creating an auto-ethnic reflective black canon with an aim of social transformation. Freedom, as a general goal and antecedent for the development of culture, the instigation of behavior, and the creation of a Black phenomenology, is the name given to a movement of people existing in a condition of forced perpetual enslavement that reduced the social status from human to African. The conceptualization of the modern era of the freedom movement ideologically allows for the placement of ideas, through a dialectical method. This methodology creates the ability for discourse in the overall movement toward freedom, by diaspora Africans in the Americas, as not only divisible into certain moments within the movement containing specific goals, but also by sharing in the general goal of freedom. These concepts were alluded to in my book *Common Ground: A Comparison of the Ideas of Consciousness in the Writings of Howard W. Thurman and Huey P. Newton*; however, in this work the description was abridged. Describing the ideas that define this subdivision serves the purpose of depicting how a philosophy of freedom was infused into to the common culture. It also demonstrates the transference of these ideas and defines the overall intellectual intentionality of the moment.

When the dissertation of W. E. B. Du Bois was published, it helped initiate a modern era of individuals who aimed the majority of their scholarly production toward the examination and explanation of human "beingness" through the lens of blackness (Black existence) with the intended purpose of creating a better lived experience. Much of this scholarly output forms the foundation of this auto-ethnic reflective canon.

Acknowledgments

The seeds of this book were planted in my first book, which was an edited version of my dissertation. The importance of this point is that it demonstrates the number of years the ideas represented here have been a part of my philosophical reflections. They have also served as points of discussion with friends, family, and colleagues for the past fourteen years. The mere mention of this also demonstrates the number of people that must be acknowledged. The late Tom Neal Jr. and Mary Frances Murphy Neal must be acknowledged first for their inspiration and the many conversations we shared during my childhood about the movement. Dr. Willette Neal, Spencer Neal, and Frances Neal have encouraged me beyond my ability to express in words. Eric Neal, you have helped me to clarify many political ideas and kept me from turning to extremes. Willie Morris Eiland and Linda Eiland, your encouragement, historical perspective, and hopefulness concerning the future keeps me grounded. I must acknowledge the personal encouragement of Jeanine Powell, Gwenita Mays, Deborah Harmon, Warren Powell, Ashley Harmon Claxton, and especially Addison Claxton, because she thinks I am a rock star because I have written a few books. Del 'Antony Campbell, the food, lodging, and tour you provided during my stay in Italy gave me time to recharge during my writing process.

Prof. Illya Davis, Dr. Stephen C. Ferguson III, Dr. Larry Perry, Dr. Melvin Rogers, Dr. Tommy Curry, Dr. Al-Yasha Williams, Dr. Gertrude Gonzales de Allen, Dr. Catherine Adams, Dr. Greg Moses, Dr. Andre Key, Dr. Dwayne Tunstall, Dr. James Edward Hackett, Dr. Emily Williams, Dr. Trenton Bailey, Dr. Walter Fluker, Dr. Luther Smith, Dr. Peter Eisenstadt, Dr. Graham Walker, thank you for being true academic friends and family. My students Mr. John Chase Bryan and Mr. Devin Hutchins, thank you for your enthusiasm.

I would like to also thank the Mississippi State University Department of Philosophy and Religion, the Shackouls Honors College, the staff of the Mitchell Memorial Library for you continued support. The Society for the Advancement of American Philosophy, Philosophy Born of Struggle, the

American Institute for Philosophical and Cultural Thought, the American Philosophical Association Session on Process Thought (especially Dr. Jea Sophia Oh and Dr. Joseph Harroff) and the Caribbean Philosophical Association for providing space for me to workshop ideas.

Lastly, the alumni brothers of the Kappa Beta Chapter of Alpha Phi Alpha Fraternity, Inc., and the Rising Star Lodge no. 282 in Weir, Ms. have both provided much-needed spiritual retreat and true friendship, especially my friend and brother, Juan Bradford.

Chapter 1

Struggling for Freedom Between Death (~~Slavery~~) and Life

Between death and life was the struggle for African American freedom.[1] Some wanted peace, some wanted revolution, but all wanted life and freedom. Slavery was death or the extinguishing of all possibility, so it was assumed that freedom had to mean having a flourishing life, a life complete with dignity and honor.[2] In these pages, what will be described is the period between slavery and freedom, between death and life, which is the modern era of the African American freedom struggle. This book should not be expected to cover every figure who is considered important, for one reason or another, to all the different people who do Black studies and African American philosophy. That is not the focus of my aim. My focus here, in part, is to examine and broaden the usual constellation of names mentioned when academics profess expertise in the study of Black people. This constellation of names is usually consistent of four or five people and never with any dissonance. Studying Black people should be like Black music or Black life. It should contain major amounts of dissonance and confusion. It should ask questions, such as the title to an Anthony Pinn book, *Why, Lord?* The struggle for freedom was abrupt and disruptive. Much that could be thought of as creating a harmonious existence was and is absent in Black life. This absence should be visible in the study of Black people. There was dissonance and polarity in their thinking, in their humanistic production, and in their actions but freedom was their aim.

    This book is not just a simple attempt to read critically the work of a Black writer or any writer for that matter, but particularly a Black writer. Nor is any other book that I have written. Reading these works critically is a noble aim to be sure, but that is not my aim. I am searching for something that is far more worthy of these precious years that I have sacrificed through graduate school and the like. Countless hours spent in libraries and archives. All this, is done so that I might be able to make a melody, as opposed to just noise. I am committed to grappling with the words lived in the modern era and not just lived during the modern era. In my weaving together the announcements of those with whom I share the experience of having been Blacked, through these attempts to understand reality and thus ease pain, I am also making the pitiful gesture of questing and questioning to see what worlds or worldviews their announcements might bring into my gaze and also the gaze of others. I am searching for the tools they made available for all who seek knowledge of how to survive deeply oppressive structures. For I realize that in this space or activity, I am not a stranger to this type of oppression, nor can I be localized or concretized to only serve as an outpouring of the prejudices others may have of me (I am not reducible to the frameworks I have been taught), because I appear a particular way to the gaze of others. My appearance is bound by the sexual choices and opportunities of my ancestors. But my ability to reason is not constricted or constrained in such a manner. Nor was the ability to reason in those of the modern era similarly constrained. It is my awareness of this very notion concerning my ability to reason that makes me an inheritor of the Black ideas that were birthed in the modern era of the African American freedom struggle. This simply means that I know that in this world, as it is currently socially constructed, it is necessary for me to reject many of the frameworks held by others if I am to come close to my potential in my becoming just as they reached the unforeseen heights achieved during the modern era. Also, as an inheritor, I am identifying as a member of a family or a people, Black people.

This book could just as well have the title *The Birth of Blackness*, but that would suggest that I intended to put forward Blackness as a singular phenomenon. This is simply not the case. The modern era of the African American freedom struggle is more in line with my intentions. The modern era became visible when W. E. B. Du Bois initiated the formal study of the Black condition of America's Black people, the former slaves of the African diaspora. This type of study, the study of Black people and their existential condition in the face of white oppression, was instigated by Du Bois as a determinant means of struggle. As the first act of this determinant struggle, Du Bois in 1896 wrote his first publication, understood here to be the beginning of the modern era of the African American Freedom Struggle, which again is the study of the Black condition. Du Bois's 1903 *The Souls of Black Folk* constructs the path (path = the writing about the Black experience) of this struggle while simultaneously putting forth the primary necessities for those engaging in the struggle posterior to him. These necessities are first to struggle reflectively upon the existential condition of Blackness in America. Du Bois expresses it in this manner, "Herein lie buried many things which if read with patience may show the strange meaning of being black here at the dawning of the Twentieth Century." In this period, other formally educated

Black Americans, just as Du Bois, aimed the majority of their scholarly production toward the examination, explanation, and expression of humanity through the lens of blackness with the intended purpose of attaining anything that could be characterized or accounted as freedom. This burgeoning ethos can be seen in what Du Bois wrote in his diary entry, as a graduate student at Harvard in 1890: "These are my plans: to make a name in science, to make a name in literature, and thus to raise my race."[3]

Secondly, necessity required that these scholars attempt to imagine the possibility of their existence absent the deep-seated oppression that is much of their experience. Howard Thurman wrote, "As long as a man has a dream in his heart he shall not lose the significance of living."[4] The world as constructed by the racist norms of whites offered very little space to participate in the notion that only whites could be fully human and all others existed at a level of humanity only nominally if at all. This construction certainly begged the question asked by Baldwin and stated here as a paraphrase, if being white provided one with the right to exploit and oppress, then isn't the notion of being white necessarily reduced or weakened to degree that the other is requisite for their fulfillment of humanity, so constructed? This unasked or rarely asked question is certainly a notion that instigated the rejection of white racist categories, making it necessary for Black people, during the modern era, to reconceptualize humanity in their image or at least inclusive thereof. In this sense, the imaginary is certainly radical, however a radical departure from existence was actually seen as a move toward reality, given that the existential was always already permanently distorted. So then, Martin Luther King Jr.'s famous speech was only far-fetched to those who believed their present to be similar to Candide, that is to say that things were as they should have been and that this was the best of all possible worlds.

Much of this scholarly output formed the foundation of an ethnic reflective canon that is useful in the understanding of the differences between the constructive philosophies which have developed within the departments of Black Studies (African American, Africana, Africana Women, Afro-American, and Africology) and those that developed within traditional departments of such disciplines as philosophy. What I take to be an ethnic reflective canon includes, but by far is not limited to, such titles as *The Souls of Black Folk* by W. E. B. Du Bois, *Discourse on Colonialism* by Aimé Césaire, *Black Skin, White Masks* by Frantz Fanon, *Jesus and the Disinherited* by Howard Thurman, *Blues People* by Leroi Jones, and *Revolutionary Suicide* by Huey P. Newton. The significance of this ethnic reflective canon has many implications, but for the purposes of this study the significance is twofold: It demonstrates an intentional effort among Black scholars and social thinkers of the modern era to participate in the movement for Black freedom through the creation of ideas and scholarly production; secondly, it demonstrates that beginning with W. E. B. Du Bois, a school of philosophical thought or critical thought developed which was constructive in purpose also countering, not correcting traditional studies, such that coexistence in traditional departments became difficult and new departments became necessary.[5]

ETHNIC REFLECTIVE CANON

The focus of this ethnic reflective canon was twofold. First, there was the intent to expand the conception of the experience of blackness over and against how it was described by others whose intent was to dehumanize through the dissemination of anti-Black racist notions. Secondly, there was the goal to advance a conception of the possibility of freedom grounded in the intense desire to experience freedom. One presupposition at work in the commitment to create this canon, which demonstrated the true depiction of being Black in the United States, was that in the aftermath of slavery if they were to experience real freedom, they would need to become a community, a Black community. In order for this community to provide the best opportunity for a flourishing future for Black people, they had to have the opportunity to know themselves in their condition and to chart their future. In other words, the ethnic reflective canon did just as Du Bois intimated. It exposed the strange meaning of Blackness in the twentieth century in words, for if we were to reframe Du Bois with a view toward gaining clarity about where the meaning of Blackness was buried, we could intuit that his statement could be expanded to announce that the meaning of Blackness was buried in his written words. For it was in his written words that upon a deep study of them, if one parsed them correctly, the humanity of Black folk became fully exposed. However, the words of the white world, in the description of Black people, were often violently oppressive. The violent and oppressive nature of these words was so pervasive that it was often told to Black schoolchildren, upon encountering horrible descriptions of Black people in their required texts, to just ignore the descriptions and search for deeper meanings. Quite frequently, the deeper meanings that were found many times were those of a damaged psyche and a sense of inferiority. A direct example of this, and the inspiration for this line of argument, is found in the poem "Incident" by Countee Cullen.[6]

Certainly physical violence, by every means imaginable, was integral to the oppression of Black people at the hands of whites, but the words of whites were sometimes just as harmful as sticks and stones. One verbal ointment for dealing with such madness was the rhyme, "Sticks and stones may break my bones, but words will never hurt me!" The poet, Countee Cullen, demonstrates verbal violence vividly in the poem about a young boys' trip to Baltimore. This idea also comes through in this reframing of the old cliché, "sticks and stones may break my bones and words, [they sometimes] hurt me." Someone reading this variation on this often-quoted cliché will quickly noticed that it has been edited to imply a particular claim instead of a universal proposition. The former universal proposition is grounded in a type of dystopian optimism usually taught to children as means of convincing them that their feelings are not as they think they are, or to put it another way, their feelings, being the product of private mental excursions, don't really matter. However, any modestly perceptive child knows that if the totality of their feelings don't indeed matter, then they themselves don't matter. Some of their feelings must matter in order for them to be a part of the world they perceive. Some people extend the dystopian version of the claim yet further, to say that the only feelings I have that matter are ones of my own choosing. This can't be true. There have to be some feelings that we have that matter beyond our choosing, especially when we consider that among the many phenomena that contain events where feelings are important, human infants are not able to choose until they develop certain cognitive abilities which aid in making choices. Therefore, feelings exist outside the purview of choice, if they exist at all. In this space, I won't attempt to make an argument for the existence of feelings, I will only rely upon neuroscientists who have developed an entire field of study that rests upon the claim that there exists the ability to collect substantive data from sensations gained through neural receptors. Some of this data collected is referred to as pain, memory, and sight. In contrast, I think that I am on solid grounding by referring to these sensations generally as feelings. So, if we can accept this claim and the claim about babies, then the ability to make a choice about which feelings matter is not requisite in order for feelings to matter. Simply put, words can be as powerful as sticks and stones. Things that can hurt me can be said to belong to the set of things that can hurt me, H = {things that can hurt me}. Sticks can hurt me. Stones can hurt me. Words can hurt me. Words do not break bones, but the pain they can cause is substantial enough such that it registers as hurting me or causing me pain.

The logic of the experience of pain associated with words can certainly be extended ad nauseam, but to make a more philosophical turn, I will now begin focusing upon what words are and how it is possible that they can hurt. Words are abstract symbols which we use to denote concepts or a conceptual picture of the world. There does exist what many refer to as the physical or phenomenal world. However, because of our human makeup, we do not have direct access to this world. We only have a conceptual understanding of this world. This conceptual understanding of the phenomenal world is the only world known by humans. It is known by humans, or to be more explicit, it is understood by humans through signs, symbols, frameworks, and experiences. Words are a part of the totality of these experiences and words also combine with the other components in the shaping of our picture or conception of the phenomenal world. In doing so, words become important. In this sense, words, collectively and individually, provide significant experiences from how we know the world and know ourselves in the world. We cannot know ourselves apart from the world. The most meaningful words are the words that shape the most meaningful parts of our world in some substantively understandable manner. Moreover, the earlier claim is still binding which intimates that this significance is not chosen by the person. This is because we are shaped and formed by our environment and the moment in which we exist; that is to say, time and space, along with feelings, make a difference in our becoming and our understanding.

Freedom and slavery are words which denote very different phenomena and are active in forming very different perceptions of the world. Dependent upon which phenomena an individual is born, their conception of the world will be formed in accordance with one of these words. Which words hurt and don't hurt also follow accordingly. They also shape the perceptual frameworks through which individuals perceive themselves in the world. Therefore, a great effort is necessary to disrupt these perceptual frameworks because disrupting these perceptual frameworks is essentially disrupting a world. They must also be replaced by another perceptual framework. Knowledge of the self is not a neutral exchange. We know ourselves in a particular world at a particular time through particular signs, symbols, frameworks, and experiences. This world also feels a particular way to us. This particularity is always contingent upon the knowledge of the knowing subject at the moment. For example, the person who is understood to be free in a given society will have a very different understanding of freedom than a person who is understood to be a slave. Certainly, time and moment even affect the meaning of slavery. So, here I must put forth that by slavery, I am concerned with the types of slavery that intentionally dehumanize.

In a world where people are intentionally dehumanized, the very act of knowing themselves as human involves a great philosophically reflective effort. To do so involves the resisting and outright rejecting of all frameworks used by the otherworld to describe them. W. E. B. Du Bois uses this notion of resisting and rejecting to begin the first chapter of his famous book *The Souls of Black Folk* by writing, "Between me and the other world."[7] This phrase recognizes the gap between his notion of himself and white people's notion of him and other Black folk. In writing this phrase, Du Bois prefigures my overarching point in this discussion. The point is oppressive institutions are hurtful to those whom they physically oppress, and the lingering perceptual frameworks, which were in part formed by the words that were used to verbally oppress during slavery, are hurtful as well. This means that even in the aftermath of slavery, the verbal oppression developed within the institution of slavery continued to remain and in certain ways still remains. In recognition of this oppressive remnant, Du Bois along with what Cedric Robinson refers to as the Black Intelligentsia, focused much of their efforts in the form of scholarly output toward vanquishing its remains. This effort was not to the exclusion of other efforts to vanquish the new forms of physical oppression. However, this text, which focuses on the modern era of the African American freedom struggle, particularly what distinguishes it and makes it modern, will also focus on the scholarly output of the Black Intelligentsia, its connective tissues, and the place it held among other efforts toward the vanquishing of oppression. In order to perform this analysis, I will rely upon a framework brought forth in my previous writings known as the freedom gaze, while also providing a more robust development of its epistemology.

FREEDOM GAZE

The freedom gaze or freedom gazing is used here to describe a perceptual framework within African American culture during the modern era stemming from the experience of the American oppressive moment. By perceptual framework, I simply mean a set of ideas or concepts people hold, which shape the way in which they view the world at such a fundamental level that it can be thought of as automatic. The freedom gaze, as a perceptual framework, can be further understood as having a perception that is framed by or filtered through the desire for freedom. In this sense, this nomenclature of freedom gaze, can be thought of as having an explanative function, one that provides an understanding and a landing from which to begin critical analyses of creative works, philosophical thoughts, and possibly even active participation within certain pursuits. The freedom gaze as a perceptual framework refers to the confluence of time, space, and moment. Moment alone can be easily misunderstood as being a synonym of time, however it is necessary to make a distinction in order to provide greater texture or a more robust description, one which narrows the focus upon a particular object of description. By using a processual hermeneutic phenomenology as an epistemological framework to gain nearness toward a meaning of perceptual framework, such as the freedom gaze, moment is meant to operate similarly to Gadamer's conception of horizon but closer to Whitehead's notion of actual occasion. In this sense, the past and the desired future must be accounted for along with the experience of the moment which can be gleaned, if only partially, by parsing the person's understanding of themselves in the context of their experiential moment.

Black ethnically reflective thinkers in the moment of the modern era took up certain themes and concerns which began to be replicated forming a cadre. Members of this cadre of ethnically reflective thinkers were also responsive to those within the cadre, whether in speeches, poetry, other works of literature, philosophical essays, and even in historical texts demonstrating an awareness of canon formation. They sometimes agreed and sometimes they disagreed. They sometimes made adjustments and at other times they used the frameworks, tropes, and analogies that were beginning to develop and extend the ongoing conversation with greater clarity. The point here, is that within the moment of the modern era, freedom gazing or the desire of these, Black ethnically reflective thinkers, for freedom as a perceptual framework fundamentally shaped their thoughts, their writings, and in many cases it shaped the activities in which they engaged. This point is made clearer through the identification of the categorical thinking which surrounded the concepts of humanity, blackness, and freedom. In a very real sense, the instability of these three concepts for Black people formed the fundamental grounding from which most of their reflections stemmed.

Certainly, there are other thinkers who address some, if not all of these categories, who were outside of this cadre and outside of those who were understood to be Black according the traditions which arose around the adjudication of *Plessy v. Ferguson*, but it was the aim of their reasoning and the respect for other Black members of the cadre which separated the members of the cadre from those who were on the outside. For example, when W. E. B. Du Bois wrote about the strange meaning of blackness at the dawning of the twentieth century and asked the question, "how does it feel to be a problem," it was certainly not a mere academic exercise.[8] The knowledge that others could only view his skin as a problem was a very real existential crisis for him as well as the "other Black boys," of which he spoke.[9] The same can be said of Howard Thurman's *Jesus and the Disinherited*. Not only did Thurman see Jesus as a member of the Disinherited, but the crisis of which he wrote was that he and others like him in the modern era were likewise members of the disinherited. It was for this group in the modern era that he wrote the book. Many on the outside could consider themselves well educated without having ever read or heard any expressions of these existential concerns by members of this cadre. Or, having heard or read one such member, felt themselves knowledgeable enough to offer solutions. These problems persist even today.

From the previously mentioned categories of humanity, blackness, and freedom, certain themes or concerns arise. The total list of concerns or themes represented would be a much longer and a more time-consuming project than is feasible for me at the moment; however, there are four of these concerns which I want to bring to the fore because in many ways they predominate in their writings and actions, therefore it would not be unfair to say that they predominated in the thoughts of those who were a part of the modern era. Because of their predominating effect, I will use them to form the conceptual framework for this project, guiding the contours of the overall discussion but also helping to make determinations about relevance in the subsections. These predominating thoughts or ideas are peace, rebellion, revolution, and freedom. These concerns are demonstrative of the nature of the resistance to the oppression which was and is experienced by Black people and the availability of the means for struggle in an ever-shifting geography of conflict. Fundamentally, the shifting geography of the struggle in which Black people participated is what for them is the Movement.

MAPPING THE MOVEMENT

People make history, but not in circumstances of their own choosing.

—Marx, 1852

Often when the idea of movement is evoked, strict attention is not given to the possibility that different understandings might exist of this term. In the absence of giving the contours of movement strict attention, there is the possibility of a failure to capture certain nuances, which leads to a reduced probability that the full intent of the word comes to the fore. On one extreme, there is the notion of movement meaning motion or the change in the spatial relationship between two or more bodies, but on another extreme there is a notion of movement meaning the exchange of ideas or change in consciousness, conceptual frameworks, or worldviews. Somewhere in between, there is the migration of feelings, emotions, the phenomenon of being in the world, or what some have labeled as a type of exchange of the self during moments of becoming. The modern era of the African American freedom struggle was certainly a movement of the people; many are in agreement concerning its existence. However, the acknowledgment of the movement is not exactly coequal to its explanation. An explanation must involve a multileveled analysis when considered, it must be kept in tension with all of the factors thought to be causal as well the agency and the very understanding of humanity that must be bound to any notion of Black people, in relation to their status as human beings, during this moment.

Some past depictions of the movement were put forward as descriptions that are totally in response to the oppressive behavior of whites. In this sense, Black people who participated in the freedom movement are not thought to have developed notions of community or even freedom which should be given any attention by today's scholars because they are believed to lack complexity and to have purported only opposition. It is at this point that I will put forth a novel understanding of freedom, one which I believe to be more useful in forming a conceptual frame from which to corral these discussions about freedom. With this conceptual framework it will be possible to gain still greater clarity about the dissonant features of the movement of blacks toward freedom and the usefulness of this analog for making these features visible. Freedom is movement. Freedom is not struggle although it may be a struggle to be free, i.e., move, but freedom and struggle are not equivalent. Freedom is simply movement and wherever there is freedom of some kind there is movement of some kind. When greater restrictions are placed upon movement of any kind, freedom is restricted to the same degree. When freedom is denied, movement is denied. The movement among Black people was about Freedom and was the exercise of Freedom. All attempts to curtail the movement were attempts to limit freedom. Therefore, to be a reactionary toward the attempts by others to gain their freedom is to be against movement which is freedom. Conservative strategies to keep things as they are limit freedom or stand against movement. Freedom is movement.

"Mapping the movement," which this section is labeled, points to an attempt to acknowledge the correlation between the concept of movement and the temporospatial reality of movement. Just as maps are used to determine location and spatial relationships at a given point in time, the idea of "mapping the movement" is meant to perform a similar function in terms of the movement. Also, just as maps use reference points to make determinations concerning these temporospatial relationships, the predominating ideas mentioned in the last section, peace, rebellion, revolution, and freedom, will also perform a similar function such that the movement can be better charted during the modern era. In order to find a location on a map there are certain tools with which one must be familiar. Of these tools, two seem to be the most important. They are coordinates and scales. For the purpose of locating an individual in terms of the geography I will make use of the following categories as coordinating tools: speeches/talks, action/activity, and writings. For the purpose of scalar quantities in terms of the coordinating categories, this analysis will use the individual's commitment to the concept, in place of numerical value, to measure their temporospatial relationship to the notion of freedom. The individual's commitment to freedom might well be verbalized and written about but they might also subscribe to the notion of peace at any cost. Their subscription to peace will put them in a position of sacrificing freedom for the sake of peace, therefore the correlation between the desire for peace and their commitment to freedom produces a low position in terms of their movement participation. No number is needed to represent this contradiction in their commitment. For example, in an attempt to quell the Los Angeles riots of the early nineties, police beating victim Rodney King, asked a now-infamous question aimed at restoring the situational stasis or peace, which existed before many witnessed his beating. King asked, "Can't we all just get along?"[10] The question, although applauded by many whites at the time, was received with disappointment and confusion by Blacks. The riots, themselves were thought to be an attempt to be heard on the way to a moment where justice could be restored.

The usage of peace, rebellion, revolution, and freedom as it applies in this writing is put forward, here and earlier, for the purpose of establishing conceptual categories and frameworks through which Black thought about the Black experience might be analyzed. In this sense, Black thought about the Black experience or Black people thinking about the existential nature of blackness is essentially philosophizing. In the performance of this reflective activity, certain common concepts have become standard notions or concepts for the comportment of Black consciousness in the face of the existential condition of blackness. Four of these concepts being peace, rebellion, revolution, and freedom, are presented here not to encapsulate all categories of Black thought, but to demonstrate African American philosophy as a distinct mode of thinking and subject of which to study. This is what I take as the point of which was presented by Lucious Outlaw in his proclamation of African American philosophy as being necessarily pragmatic in character while focusing on the existential conditions of Black people.[11] To be sure, this type of thought or philosophizing can be separated into two modes or forms, one formal and the other informal. The purpose here is not to determine which is the more valid mode, but to demonstrate that Black people have systematically thought about the Black experience and have even gone further to also think about how one should think the Black experience. Certainly, I do not mean to propose that eventually writings or texts will be found on plantation archeological digs containing the philosophical musings of the formerly enslaved Africans. I simply mean that the activity known as philosophizing was not foreign to Black people, but it was not until the modern era that opportunities to put these thoughts on paper presented themselves in any significant measure. Peace, rebellion, revolution, and freedom serve as guideposts such that upon mapping the movement, the contours of such philosophizing might easily become, in the words of Charles Mills, "Blackness Visible."

An early example approaching what is meant by the notion currently being put forward, is demonstrated in the writings of Frederick Douglass. In his, "Oration, Delivered in Corinthian Hall, Rochester, July 5, 1852," Douglass asked, "What, to the American slave, is your Fourth of July?" The implication of the question assumes that at least some of the currently enslaved possessed, at the time of the speech, the ability to think about the meaning of this particular holiday for themselves. This essentially means that they thought about what thoughts they had on the matter, in other words they thought of themselves thinking about this American special day or it can be said that they philosophized. Evidence of this phenomenon is demonstrated by Douglass, who himself was a former slave. As Douglass resolved to throw light on the matter through the writing of this speech, methodologically it was not necessary for him to appeal to the phenomenological renderings of qualitative research provided by way of interviews with other former slaves. He knew firsthand how an enslaved person might feel, for he had once suffered that very fate, except now he could place his thoughts into words. He was able to reflect on his own past thoughts on the matter. He was also able to make determinations about their meaning. In doing so, extrapolations as to what his thoughts implied could be made. Douglass states, "To him [the American slave], your celebration is a sham." This statement was made immediately after asking what these celebrations meant to the American slave. He does not equivocate in using such a description. This description is a demonstration that in reflecting upon his thoughts as a slave, Frederick Douglass reflected upon the occurrence of these celebrations, observed their contradictions, and was able to make a determination about the meaning and value of the same. Also, in this thought process or the philosophizing of Douglass, the recognition that the reflective act was catalytic in changing the slave in terms of how he came to understand the concept of American freedom and his own feelings on the matter was evident. It exposed to Douglass that he could not consider the celebration to be about freedom while so many were still in bondage.

Certainly, Frederick Douglass would count as a participant in the freedom movement, although outside or before the modern era. Meaning he was conceptually outside of the bounds of the modern era and existed before timeframe and existential conditions which brought about the modern era. He was bound by custom which addressed his blackness, but he was never bound by the adjudication of *Plessy v. Ferguson*. There was no national legal standard which separated his skin from others. But what is Douglass's relationship to the freedom movement? In other words how can it be demonstrated through points of reference that Douglass, Alain Locke, and even Howard Thurman were in the same social movement without singularly referencing the obvious commonality of race, which in this sense becomes a weak reference tool? Narrowly speaking, a movement or the participants in a movement, and therefore the nonparticipants as well, can be classified in relationship to the movement by their psychology or conscious thought concerning the movement, their activity (e.g., grassroots organizing) with respect to the movement, or their humanistic expression created in support of the movement or spawned by the agenda of the movement. An example of this would be Angela Davis, Fannie Lou Hamer, and Elizabeth Catlett, each of whom were members of the Freedom Movement within the modern era. Angela Davis is recognized as a scholar whose writings demonstrate a revolutionary mindset or consciousness. Fannie Lou Hamer was recognized as a grassroots organizer and leader who help found the Mississippi Freedom Party. Elizabeth Catlett, on the other hand, was a revolutionary artist who had her citizenship revoked for her activities as an artist. These three each represent one of the classifications and the necessity of their placement within the movement can also be clearly demonstrated.

The demonstration of placement within the movement will be performed later in the book using the method of mapping the movement mentioned previously. However, before the mapping function can be fully explored, the predominating ideas of peace, rebellion, revolution, and freedom must be defined in terms of their intended use and their relevance indicated as it pertains to this work. The defining of these terms is necessary because of the recognition that their regular usage is fraught with ambiguity and inaccuracies leading to relativistic and situational understandings. These understandings allow individuals to think of them in terms of their own proclivities. I will begin with peace and build toward the a consistent conceptual framework in which to situate the other terms. Peace assumes the reasonable attainment of an acknowledged common good. Common good can be understood, in this sense, as an established flourishing environment for the greater community. However, just as there is the concept of peace, there is also a negative or false notion of peace, which is understood to be only the absence of verbal and physical conflict. An understanding of this negative notion of peace is required in order to deconstruct or rupture an often used but terribly inadequate notion of the term. The inadequacy in this notion of peace stems from an assumption that certain things are held common, such as a common effort toward the goal of peace along with common or shared notions about what counts as the flourishing experience. Peace as an ideal obtains relevance within social contexts owing to its connection to the concept of the good or a flourishing life. A life that flourishes in this context has no essential meaning but must be kept in tension with concepts such as expansion, progress, growth, and fulfillment. These concepts are usually thought to be opposite to a fragile existence or a life full of disappointment. Conceptually, since the meaning that is provided here for peace is understood to be fundamentally communal, I have therefore provided a meaning for flourishing which is also attached to community.

Whereas peace should be understood to be necessarily communal or an agreement between two or more, rebellion requires no such agreement. Rebellion, as such, occurs when the authority or majority no longer provides for the common good or no longer establishes a flourishing environment. Rebellion in this sense should be understood as an overt act of rejection, by an individual or group, of the predominant ideas or power structure which hinder the opportunities for flourishing by a group within the larger community or by an individual. Rebellion is demonstrated by simply saying no, or it can also be a complex planned maneuver to demonstrate disagreement. However, rebellion begins by freely thinking, particularly thinking which is in opposition to the authority or larger communal structure. Thus, rebellion is a process which begins in meaningful silence. Rebellion is also the first step in a social movement. By comparison, peace stops social movement or thwarts its beginning. Rebellion requires social consciousness or some thought about the self in relationship to the power structure or larger group. It is plausible that peace does not carry the same requirement, because thought about peace is less concerned with difference and more concerned with commonality. The more a person is committed to peace, their commitment to rebellion rises to the opposite degree. Therefore, even nonviolent struggle cannot be fully equated to peace, because of its requirement to struggle. This is because struggle requires resistance in some fashion, nonviolent struggle is also a type of rebellion. Peaceful resistance or peaceful struggle are both corrupted concepts or misleading propaganda with no clear and concise meaning. Resistance and struggle are both rebellious actions and both are meant to disrupt peaceful states of existence. Therefore, rebellion tugs at the very fiber of peace. The references made to a "peaceful" rebellion must therefore be taken as referencing the tactics of the rebellion and not to maintenance of the status quo.

Revolution is often confused with rebellion, but unlike rebellion, revolution requires a shared decision to make change, after which action is taken. Revolution rises above mere resistance or the mere resistive act and is indicative of communal thinking and communal effort to bring about societal change in consciousness coupled with substantive structural changes. Revolutionaries do not seek only to resist the status quo; revolutionaries desire to change the status quo. Also, because revolution requires that the revolutionary go beyond mere rebellion by developing a change of consciousness or philosophical thinking and deep structural changes, it is therefore a higher or more intense form of rebellion. The revolutionary is compelled to not only consciously dissent, reject, or refuse; but, the revolutionary must consider what the new beginning or way forward entails. This is the philosophical component. They must consider what constitutes the change they seek and what is only a reform of the status quo. The creation formed or the substance of the revolution, in some fundamental way, must be incongruent with the previous instantiation of that society. If this is not true, can we really think that a revolution has occurred? Who gets to decide? It must be the revolutionary, of course. The answer to the question has much to do with the true form of peace mention earlier. First, it was established that peace assumes the reasonable attainment of an acknowledged common good. Next, peace was established to be necessarily communal or an agreement between two or more. Revolutionaries engage in the revolutionary act because they cannot flourish or positively develop, which stifles their humanity. "The right to development is a fundamental human right that lies at the intersection of the entire gamut of economic, social cultural, political and civil rights."[12] To develop is basic to all biological life, but for humans development, at least on some level, requires agency. Agency requires freedom. Accordingly, revolution is thus the assertion of agency where freedom has been denied. Therefore, the peace that the revolutionary desires is commensurate with freedom.

INTEREST IN THE SUBJECT

Social thinkers from many disciplines have made tremendous strides toward the goal of providing a synoptic or systematic view from which to understand the Black or African diaspora experience in the Americas and otherwise. Their efforts have instigated a certain understanding in me of what was the strange meaning of blackness in the modern era. As a humanistically focused philosopher, I find it necessary to constantly reframe and reformat my understanding of what being human really is because of my existence in a moment when society continues to classify me as a Black man. One means of approaching a *eureka* moment in this quest is to make an attempt to discover the limits of human possibility. Another means is to examine the means by which humans band together to overcome the obstacles. No one has more obstacles than those of the oppressed, which means making the study of the oppressed necessary, particularly for the knowledge of how to overcome oppression as a fundamental obstacle for humans when cultures clash. In a study such as this, the formation of culture and social networking coupled with the effects of temporospatial dynamics are essential in the development of a schema for interrogating these means for approaching the eureka moment. Although this moment may never be fully attained, the subsequent investigative experience does provide a useful glimpse from which some assertions can be made.

Some early examples of these strides are *The Negro's God: As Reflected in His Literature* by Benjamin Elijah Mays, *Negro Voices in American Fiction* by Hugh Morris Gloster, *The Black Vanguard: Origins of the Negro Social Revolution* by Robert Hughes Brisbane. Each of these works approaches their study using the differing disciplinary tools gained specifically from their academic training to help approach the meaningfulness of the Black experience as cast in America. This is evidenced by their use of the term "Negro" as an identifying marker for the subjects of their studies. There is also evidence that the aim of each author was to attempt to capture something of the Black mind, that is some part of what is was to be Black in the modern era of the African American freedom struggle. The significance of these attempts rests on their demonstrations of the humanity of Black people in America in a universal sense while also providing a descriptive analysis of the uniqueness of the oppressive moment in the United States. This uniqueness has much to do with the reluctance of the white majority residing in the United States to acknowledge the humanity of these Black people through public policies, common human courtesies, and the acknowledged presupposed ideological belief of these whites in the equality of all humans, which is exposed in the Declaration of Independence. In the text by Mays, we find shifts in the conception of God as the existential conditions of Black life shifted. The text by Gloster demonstrates that the mind of Black people was not a mind that was simply molded by whites or even an imitation of whites, but a unique development of the racial consciousness of the day combined with the pressures of anti-Black racism. Lastly, Brisbane makes apparent the coalescing of a Black effort through organizations such as the Urban League and the NAACP to beat back (Booker T.) Washingtonian ideology while also providing a collective front against the combined white American effort from both the North and the South to the dehumanize Black citizens through public policy and political action. These works epitomize the shift in the methods during the modern era of Black social thinkers becoming educated and focusing this education to determine meaning and problem of blackness.

Some contemporary examples of continuing attempts to make even more deliberate strides are *Prophesy Deliverance: An Afro-American Revolutionary Christianity* by Cornel West, *Blues, Ideology, and Afro-American Literature: A Vernacular Theory,* by Houston A. Baker Jr. and *The Black Atlantic: Modernity and Double Consciousness* by Paul Gilroy. These works demonstrate a deep rootedness within the tradition that was developed by the earlier authors, but also portend to the shifting nuances in certain understandings of Black beingness to meet the changing existential conditions. One of the nuances is the increasing prevalence of the replacement of the term Negro with the terms Afro-American or Black. These attempts at self-definition focus on addressing the acknowledgment of a historical relationship with Africa and also capturing the increased immigration to the United States by other members of the African diaspora. Cornel West's effort in his text was committed to making an aspirational move toward outlining a normative conception the Black (Revolutionary) Christian tradition at its best. To do this he charted the history of the movement as he saw it, while pointing out why this tradition, above all other ideologies, is necessary for the future survival of Black people. The text by Houston Baker Jr. is profound owing to its attempt to further earlier claims made by writers such as Amiri Baraka that the proper metaphoric signifier of the second ordered experience of experiencing Black culture or reflecting upon Black culture is the blues or what he termed the blues matrix.[13] He also determined it to be a fundamentally American vernacular experience. In order to achieve this aim, several texts were used to determine and trace the African American vernacular experience in its literary form and as it shifted over time, while also being mindful of the interstices it shares with the broader American vernacular also as found in literature. In doing so, he found that African American vernacular culture was intertwined with American culture and that the reverse was true as well.

Paul Gilroy's *The Black Atlantic* attempts to reach beyond the veneer of the Black experience in order to make a new determination about the way in which culture, i.e., people groupings, are constructed. He posits that cultures are not formed according to national or even international borders, but that there is overlapping and a cross-pollenating process such that the finished product has stitched within its tapestry multiple colors and patterns. The effect of this line of thought renders what Gilroy labels as a Black Atlantic culture instead of an African American, Caribbean, Afro-British culture. The upshot of this line of thought seems to be that there is a way to capture the appearance of a Black person from Mississippi who wears dreadlocks, and loves listening to reggae music. While this seems to account for a certain cultural spread, I am not sure that the same process could not be captured, albeit even awkwardly, by the term Pan African. In consideration of the gains for this idea, and to measure if they can truly be called such, an assessment of what is lost should be of concern as well. The necessity to perform this task for the Gilroy book and not for the other book mentioned above has to do with his intentional changing of the frame of reference through which to view Black people and their cultures. It seems that what is lost or at least thrown into flux is the idea that mainstream or popular cultures began as the bedrock ideas of folk cultures. Gilroy seems to rest the culture creating process with the mainstream or even the elite grouping. I don't disagree that there is always cross-pollination; however, I remain unconvinced that there exists a Black Atlantic subject. I would not strip away, conceptually, the Black Atlantic world. I would simply suggest that the Black Atlantic world contained subjects that could only experience a more immediate framing with a diluted effect when the experiencing radius is increased.

Even if Gilroy's thesis is flawed, *The Black Atlantic* makes an important contribution in terms of what things about other spaces must be considered when the African American Freedom Struggle is considered. I have used the term flawed here, after taking Gilroy at his word, to demonstrate the problematics of abstracting the notion of what it means to be Black from its temporal spatial reality. Gilroy clearly speaks to his desire to rise above the nationalist and even essentialist notions of being Black. In order to do so, an abstract construct is created to treat all blackness of certain moment within its conceptual frame. This conceptual frame is the Black Atlantic. However, when this frame is implemented, immediately what must be considered is what is essential qualities are jettisoned in favor of the new conception. Also, what should be considered is the relevance, reasonableness, or nearness of the abstracted frame to the reality being of Black in the particular. Although it could be considered good to create such an abstract concept which rises above essentialism and nationalism; however, this should always be weighed against damage done to notions developed from real world data. The existence and use of real world data may give the impression of a nationalist bias, but impressions can and often are mistaken. Whenever theories run counter to evidentiary claims based upon research, then any debt to the theorists must be canceled in favor of reassessing. Sometimes there is a good place for abstraction, but sometimes there is not.

There is a challenge put forward by Adolph Reed Jr. in his book *Stirrings in the Jug*. This challenge is to scholars, who's desire it is to advance emancipatory and egalitarian interests in Black political life. They must "look within the jug," a metaphor used previously by Ralph Ellison. In this attempt to perform an analysis of the modern era, I am interested in engaging in this same activity, similar to the way Reed imagines it, but for the purposes of capturing any ideas capable of advancing modes of thought that can assist in developing a clearer picture concerning the progress and goals of the Black struggle for freedom. In doing so, I hope to demonstrate the value of reflective thinking for the goal of flourishing as a human.[14]

NOTES

1. Several allusions are at work in this sentence. One is to the title from the book by Bill Lawson and Howard McGary, *Between Slavery and Freedom* and the idea of slavery as social death found in the book by Orlando Patterson, *Slavery and Social Death*. The reference to death arises from Orlando Patterson's determination of slavery as being a social death. Angela Davis; however, refers to freedom as a lifetime of struggle or requires struggle to maintain. Angela Y. Davis, *Freedom is a Constant Struggle* (London: Penguin Books, 2021); Bill E. Lawson and Frank M. Kirkland, *Frederick Douglass: A Critical Reader* (Malden, MA: Blackwell); Orlando Patterson, *Freedom. Vol. 1* (New York: Basic Books, 1996).

2. Ibid.

3. David L. Lewis, *W. E. B. Du Bois: A Reader* (New York: H. Holt, 1995), p. 3.

4. Howard Thurman, *Meditations of the Heart* (Boston: Beacon, 1953), p. 36.

5., Reiland Rabaka, *W. E. B. Du Bois and the Problems of the Twenty-First Century: An Essay on Africana Critical Theory* (Lanham, MD: Lexington Books, 2017), pp. 2–15.

6. In the poem, "Incident" by Countee Cullen, there was an exchange between two young boys, one Black and one white, in which the social epithet used by the white child stymied the Black child's ability to experience joy during his summer vacation. Countee Cullen and Gerald Lyn Early. *My Soul's High Song: The Collected Writings of Countee Cullen, Voice of the Harlem Renaissance* (New York: Anchor Books).

7. W. E. B. Du Bois, *Du Bois' Writings*, (New York: The Library of America), p. 363.

8. Ibid, p. 363.

9. Ibid, p. 364.

10. "When LA Erupted In Anger: A Look Back At The Rodney King Riots," NPR, accessed March 21, 2022, https://www.npr.org/2017/04/26/524744989/when-la-erupted-in-anger-a-look-back-at-the-rodney-king-riots

11. Phillip McReynolds, "The Pragmatism of Black Folk," *American Philosopher* #32, July 31, 2013, http://youtu.be/OPQdQ7M0kHo

12. Wilfred L. David, "The Human Right to Development," *Philosophy and African Development,* Lasana Keita, ed. (CODESRIA: Dakar, Senegal), p. 37.

13. Amiri Baraka was later followed by Houston Baker in the use of the blues matrix.

14. Through the use of the nomenclature reflective thinking, it is simply meant philosophical inquiry. However, in order to gain the most robust nature and the true intent of this nomenclature, it best understood as meaning professional specialized academic philosophical inquiry. In this sense, consideration is given to the categorical nature of the claims being made, the arguments of all possible valid interlocutors, assumed necessary commitments, and extrapolated implications. The widest possible net was cast that would continue to provide a narrowly focused relevant argument such that the implications created might be meaningful to concerned thinkers about the Black experience in the modern era of the African American freedom struggle. Adolph L. Reed, *Stirrings in the Jug: Black Politics in the Post-Segregation Era* (Minneapolis: University of Minnesota Press, 1999), pp. 51–52.

Chapter 2

The New Negro's Negritude

W. E. B. DU BOIS AS EXEMPLAR

Negritude is a French term which was literally co-opted from a French root that had a derogatory connotation. Students of African descent matriculating at the Sorbonne in the late 1930s repurposed the root term to mean blackness or to refer to people of African descent. However, in the use of the repurposed form, there was the notion that certain essential qualities of blackness could be taken for granted. The term is used here as demonstration of its inherent ambiguity along with the same quality being found in the term blackness and being Black. The experience of blackness is not the same as being Black. Both are ambiguous owing to the lack of historical grounding, leaving the meanings of each to be determined by the perception of the user. The phrases are usually stated with such convenience that the idea or mental picture these phrases engender have no real world attachment to any set of cultural values or material conditions of which all associated could agree. It was a goal of Du Bois to attempt to bring clarity to this the concept of blackness. Any serious research on the subject of blackness should at minimum seek to expose the meaning in an explicit manner such that the intended meaning can be understood by the general reader.

Since October 1, 2019, after applying for early promotion and in order to thoroughly demonstrate evidence of my long-term commitment to research, I immediately began new projects, further extending what I see as the goal of bringing clarity to African American philosophy or philosophy of the Black experience proper. To this end, I have authored an article and solicited a call for papers in order to compose a special edition of the journal *The Acorn: Philosophical Studies in Pacifism and Nonviolence*, of which I am listed as the guest editor. The significance of this article entitled, "New Directions for the Study of King and Thurman,"[1] is that it casts light upon the importance of philosophy of the Black experience while simultaneously casting light on the entirety of my project to this point. African American philosophy or philosophy of the Black experience seeks to discover definitions, categories, and the existential conditions of blackness, but also to provide a rigorous and robust treatment of the same, especially where none exists. The intent in doing this is not only one of discovery, but to put forth empirical as well as normative claims useful in addressing hindrances to whatever qualifies as a flourishing life. This project is Du Boisian in nature, not as a sociological study, but a phenomenological one in the tradition of *The Souls of Black Folk*, determining a robust meaning of blackness during the modern era of the African American Freedom Struggle and beyond. The capturing of the meaning of blackness during this or any period has import for future studies of Black people, whether these studies be philosophical, scientific, literary or otherwise. By making these distinctions in this multiplicity that is understood as Black people, the same can be understood in terms that are discreet and continuous. This helps to identify significant changes in their existential conditions while continuing to be able to maintain certain referential commitments. However, since other peoples around the world have experienced similar oppressive conditions, further import is applicable universally to all oppressed cultures.

This chapter begins the first step toward investigating the components of Reed's jug mentioned in the last chapter. Attempting to meet the challenge put forward by Reed requires the acknowledgment of certain assumptions concerning the ability to analyze and assess the experience of the moment and the modes of thought, otherwise known as the development of consciousness. The significance of analyzing the experience of the moment, or the experiential moment, has much to do with the emphasis that I wish to place on the development of humans, generally speaking, and the development or particular persons or cultures. First, how does the experiential moment happen? Next, when does the experiential moment take place? And finally, what evidence exists to suggest that the scheme being depicted, that there exists the ability to analyze and assess the experiential moment, is a likely scenario? In order to demonstrate a resistant attitude toward my own presuppositions, these questions require an attempt to understand precisely not only what is being asked, but also what kinds of questions are being asked in order to determine what kind of answer might be best fitted for such a question. It is imperative to acknowledge at the onset that the description of the experiential moment is not an exact science and that the concern here is with the ability to bring precision to the description of the experiential moment and therefore to show with the greatest probability of the actuality of its existence. An approximation of the actual experiential moment is an acceptable end. The realization that all moments are undeniably bound to other moments is not being disputed. However, the ability to use abstraction as a tool of human reason for the purpose of analysis does provide an opportunity to form an approximated description. The development into particular persons or cultures is also largely linked to an awareness of the self as an individual, and is based on perception, or knowledge of experience. Therefore, the answers to the previous questions of how, when, and what, are tied to, or are reliant upon knowledge in a very foundational manner.

The what question, which is certainly epistemic in nature, seems to me to present the most important information, but it also seems to represent the simplest answer.[2] However simple it may be, its simplicity in no way reduces its importance. This question or this type of question shines a light on the flawed Cartesian cogito conception,[3] because of its basic implication that if he was a thinking thing, then it would be possible to perform such thinking in a vacuum, thinking of nothing. However, it is not through cognitive ability, particularly in the reflective form, that we enter into the physical world with all of its physical and temporal restraints. We enter this world through sensory perception. Cognition or thinking is the act we perform when attempting to interpret or ascribe meaning to an event experienced through the senses. Sensory perception precedes cognitive ability in development. Humans develop certain responses and reflex actions that correspond to our sensory perceptions of which cognitive ability, especially in the form of reflective thought, is only one among many. Therefore, to discover ourselves as a thinking thing is to discover ourselves somewhere, at some moment in time, thinking about something, all of which is analyzable. If the full extrapolation of the Cartesian dubito were to be applied, then it could not exclude the act of thinking itself. To do so would be to alter the very meaning of the foundational term, cognition. The base meaning, to think or to form a mental a picture, always requires an object. In fact, Descartes's inversion of the proper order in which we come to know the world and ourselves in the world creates the fatal flaw. Descartes reframes the human as a thinking being that has sense perceptions or can feel.[4] The actual order of human experience is that we are feeling beings that have reason or cognition and can use reason to analyze and synthesize our sensory perceptions, making our reality a coherent one. To be sure, there are limits to this process but our approximations make our analyses and syntheses useable.

Experiential Moments

As it was written in my first book, in order to study consciousness, we must study its effect.[5] This is done by observing patterns of behavior, reactions to phantasms,[6] and the development of signs, symbols, and frameworks. This all comes together to determine clues from which to analyze and define subjective experience or individual consciousness. Although, the instructive force of a directive such as studying the effect of consciousness is partially explanative of the process; it does fall short of providing an explanation for the development of the interpretation of being which could be taken to mean essence but should also be understood to rely on consciousness or the interpretation of subjective experience. Once this subjective experience is defined, it can then be categorized. The method I have chosen to extensively analyze the effect that the experiential moment had on the consciousness of Black people in general, and specifically Black people in the modern era more explicitly considered, is to critically examine their existential judgement of the experiential moment of the modern era. My choice in this matter is reliant upon my consideration of this method to be the only useful method for the performance of this task. This method is consistent with the manner in which humans perform the task of cognition in reference to experience generally, and in some measure, from moment to moment throughout their conscious life.

Now it is necessary to respond to the previous first question, responded to here secondly, which was how does the experiential moment happen? In answering this question, I will make an effort to explain experiential moments as they pertain to blackness. This will demonstrate the importance of the possibility for a singular experiential event or set of multiple experiential events being relevant and meaningfully responsible for the shaping of a unique people or culture. A variety of considerations must immediately come to the fore, in order that the active process of this moment can be clearly understood. These range from the temporospatial positioning, sociopolitical conditions, existential concerns, to the perceptual frameworks learned and used as tools of interpretation. Initially the definition of experiential moment will be exposed, beginning with simple terms, and then expanded, such that the definitional clarity gained will create enough space for this conceptual notion to add the greatest amount of force to the ancillary ideas being associated.

The experiential moment is the moment when we become aware of an intelligible object through our senses and we also become simultaneously intellectually aware of the same object. We have no experience of the things we do not sense in this manner. The things that are not sensed in this manner are non-sensed objects to the human. The possibility of the things which can be experienced through our senses and our rational faculties include persisting ideas,[7] objects, and qualities which objects possess.[8] When objects are sensed in this manner, the function of reason or the intellect is to raise the sensory awareness of an object, or that which is intelligible, to the point of knowledge. This is an immediate event in that the object which is knowable is known the moment it is perceived. Of course, there is always room for the improvement or clarity of knowledge, but the fact remains that the object is known the moment it moves from possibility of knowledge to actual knowledge, which also speaks to the status of the knower as a knower of something.

As it pertains to being Black, particularly in its connection to the modern era, the significance of the experiential moment is found in how this process unfolds. Being Black is a shifting set of cultural performances produced by the experience of being Black at a particular moment in time. It is very much a product of the lived experience. There is not now and has there ever been an essence attached to what it means to be Black that is formed exterior to the lived experience of blackness. Because there is no essence, the individual has to come the knowledge of blackness on their own. The other factors mentioned above (temporospatial positioning, sociopolitical conditions, existential concerns, the perceptual frameworks learned and used as tools of interpretation) become determinate factors in what a knower knows when they come to possess the knowledge of blackness.

The experiential moment of blackness is also what gave energy to the claim in *Common Ground*⁹ that community development and social transformation might be possible grounded in the consciousness derived from the shared experience of the phenomenon which was being blacked by law and oppressed because of the color of one's skin or the color of one's ancestor's skin. In that work, which was my freshman book, the argument used did not clearly bring to the fore the sense in which I was developing the notion of blackness as resulting from an existential moment of experience. This created the problem of portraying blackness as an inner essence, as opposed to it coming about in the physical world under certain temporospatial conditions. These temporospatial conditions give way to the experience of being bound by the social constriction which is blackness. It is the social constriction which forces one into a community, whether physically or ideological. The community is based upon the perceptual frameworks that develop within and without those who are blacked by law and custom, such that a sense of who Black people are is held by Black people and others. This shared sense of what it means to be Black or white for that matter, which is only an approximation, is what was meant by the idea of a shared consciousness in *Common Ground*. It was thought by many Black thinkers during the modern era, that if Black people were clearer through approximations concerning the real experience of oppression felt by the average Black person, then they would fight harder for social transformation. More will be said about the dissipation of this sentiment toward the end of the modern era, but suffice to say that the experiential moment of blackness served as a gravitational pull many felt within the Black community.

It was 1940, when Du Bois was seventy-two years of age, that he exclaimed he had essayed for half a century "thoughts centering around the hurts and hesitancies that hem the [Black people] in America." However, there was one experiential moment that stood out for Du Bois, in spite of the many profundities of which a person of Du Bois's statue most certainly would have had to experience. But, Du Bois's recording of this experience, in the pages of *Dusk of Dawn,* stands as a demonstration that many of the contours of the Black experience can neither be eloquently described or rationally explained. They can only be presented with their exhausting comments about the experiential moment, reluctantly and slowly, following. For many, the Black experience in America is fraught with the contingent possibility of a tragic occurrences ladened with the strong prospect of being the catalyst for substantial shifts in the experiencers lived experience. When a specific experiential moment of Du Bois's is mentioned, it serves the dual intent of exposing his reflective thoughts via his writings, which in turn exposes him, as one among other Black people, affected by this added fragility incurred from being Black while living in an anti-Black society.

Post-confrontation, Du Bois faced a conclusive moment of self-realization with considerations which forever altered the direction or aim of Du Bois's focus. The first realization: one could not be a calm, cool, and detached scientist while Negroes were lynched, murdered and starved;[10] reveal his future disposition and comportment to his subject matter. The second consideration: there was no such definite demand for scientific work of the sort that [he] was doing; foreshadowed the close proximity and tension that Du Bois would maintain between value and fact.[11] The tension became necessary owing to Du Bois's realization that it was not simply a lack of understanding about basic human potential that kept Black people in an inferior societal position. This positioning was tied to the very aim of white political policy where individuals racialized as Black were the focus. The claim could be made that the impact of this moment upon Du Bois might here be exaggerated, since Du Bois only devoted two paragraphs to the scenario. While it is true that only two paragraphs were thus composed for the retelling of the scenario, Du Bois would spend much of a long life with this moment as a guiding cloud. This is evidenced by recounting the fact that in 1940, when *Dusk of Dawn* appeared, Du Bois is seventy-two years of age, which is forty-one years removed from the actual moment.[12] Regardless, of the space allocated for the explicit depiction of the matter, it was this moment's effect upon Du Bois and the subsequent dedication to the depiction of "the strange meaning of being black," which could be described as an existential turn, that reveals the impact of this moment. Du Bois's realization that science alone could not account for the phenomenological constriction of Black people by the white establishment required a different type of framing of which a scientific account, with its analytic tools, struggles to achieve.

This was not the first such experience of which Du Bois made mention. The first such mentioning of this type of experiential moment was listed in *The Souls of Black Folk*, which, as Du Bois wrote in the forethought, was part and parcel of the strange meaning of being Black in the dawning of the twentieth century. In the first chapter, Du Bois exposes the experience of existing as a pathological being, or simultaneously as a question and answer to the major problem of an era. Along with performing this task, he envelops his coming to knowledge of his own blackness and what this knowledge meant for him, making the reader also shoulder the weight of blackness, if only for a moment, to at least make an attempt at understanding what was the meaning of blackness at the dawning of Du Bois's century. According to Du Bois, the "shadow swept across"[13] him when he was just a boy, during his early years in Great Barrington, Massachusetts. It was in his description of the of the card exchange, which for him was the annunciation of his blackness, where we find an unfolding of the problematic attached to the experiential moment of discovery. In this moment, one from which Du Bois could never turn away, the realization that there existed a veil, or a wall even, beyond which Du Bois and "the darker boys"could not participate. He also seemed to know immediately, although this knowledge certainly would increase with greater intensity in the years to come, that the existence of this wall set a limit for all Black people. This limit reduced, for all people racialized as Black and living in America, the freedoms of which were so boldly encapsulated in the Declaration of Independence. Being limited in this way was certainly a reduction in his freedom. Freedom in this sense was now clearly seen, by Du Bois and others from whom it was denied, as a requirement for human fulfillment and therefore it was as much a part of their philosophical concerns as well as their existential concerns. Freedom not only made one experience full humanity, but it also is among the most important determinants of the way in which humans see reality. To not have freedom in a society where others are free makes one constantly a freedom gazer.[14] About this Du Bois stated, "It would not do to concenter all effort on economic well-being and forget freedom and [humanity] and equality."[15] Such was the evident motivating factor of Du Bois's life's work. Du Bois charted this claim in his three-volume ethnographic work[16] which he claims to have centered on "the hurts and hesitancies that hem the Black [humanity] in America."[17] It is demonstrably clear that Du Bois saw the lack of any measurable freedom as an existential crisis for Black people.

DuBois's Existential Crisis

In *Dusk of Dawn*, in order to determine a true account of a legal matter involving a Southern Georgia Black man, named Sam Hose, Du Bois recounts his objective in using applied science, which he believed to be the determining factor in paradigmatic shifts of value and subsequently changes in political policy. Du Bois briefly recounts his desire to use science, understood here as a disciplined system or method used for the pursuit of a particular truth,[18] to generate within whites a confrontation with irrefutable facts, that upon being exposed, a change in attitude, in terms of legal adjudication of guilt verses vigilante justice, might be possible. Once Du Bois had determined the best approximation of the matter, it was his intent to deliver the information to the newspaper of record in Atlanta, where he was located; however, before this became possible Du Bois was himself confronted with a different type of truth. This truth had to do with the essential nature found in one of his experiential moments framed as an encounter with blackness as constructed in the modern era of the freedom struggle. This experiential encounter was a type of negritude,[19] although differently cast than the negritude of the later cultural movement, nonetheless, it exemplified a fragile essence of Black life existing at a moment in space just beyond the bounds of the self-evident truths Thomas Jefferson so eloquently penned, which are all were created equal and as such were born with unalienable rights that could be conflated as exhibiting freedom. These rights were said to be self-evident, meaning any reasonable minded person should reach the same conclusion. The absence of any semblance of these rights applied to Black people, during Du Bois's moment and before, seems to suggest that whites were not reasonable minded in their dealings with their darker skinned counterparts.

Legally, Black people were free; however, legal statutes require enforcement. Even the announcement from Thomas Jefferson was clear that freedom required the intervention of government. His statement, "That to secure these rights, governments are established among men," is meant to offer the suggestion that the possibility for the existence of rights without enforcement is negligible. Be that as it may, America had a government from 1776 forward, and yet, Black people had no rights that white people were being governed to respect. By 1896, there seemed to be some progress made; however, life, without which the other rights are but mere breaths wasted, was not secure by the government for Black people. Du Bois was attempting to use reason to reconcile this dilemma, but to no avail, for reason requires that there exists some agreed upon commonality. A foundational notion, which the rejection thereof halted the possibility of forward progress in terms of human relations between Blacks and whites, was the disbelief in the idea that Black people were as human as white people. This nonacceptance by white people stymied nearly one hundred years of forward progress for Black people in America. So the Black person could legally be free, but legal without government enforcement is merely theoretical. The problem Black people faced in America was an existential crisis and not theoretical one. The hindering of Black people's natural development, in terms of material conditions,[20] by whites thwarted many of the opportunities Black people had for a flourishing life, inclusive of freedom.

Until 1899, Du Bois's writings could in many ways be reduced to, or could be equated to but not more than the sum of his education, by his own admission. This does not mean that he took up his professors' problems or shared their major concerns. These assumptions would simply mean that his writings demonstrated frameworks consistent with the whole or some part of his academic training. These writings began in the year 1896 with the publication of Du Bois's dissertation[21] *The Suppression of the African Slave Trade to the Americas* and also includes *The Philadelphia Negro*. However, after 1899, no longer would Du Bois depend solely upon analyses and supporting commentaries as a way of healing the Negro problem. Du Bois realized that if the problem were to have more than a theoretical solution, clarity was not enough. This problem prompted Du Bois's turn toward being a scholar and activist.[22] It would also require the acknowledgment that the frameworks within which he was trained constrained the unsuspecting scholar to a certain version of reality consistent with the racist findings of other scholars. Du Bois no longer depended on any system reliant only upon law and reason. He did not jettison the rigor of scientific thought; however, he realized that there was no connection between scientific conclusions about the world and the ethical values scientists and philosophers would use, to produce the world of their desires. Science only provided the means for which to bring this iteration of the world into being, technologically speaking. What Du Bois saw in the continuing unfolding of the world scheme, which was driven by the powerful, was that it seemed to allow for more exploitation and more oppression.

This was both an epistemic and an existential crisis for Du Bois at once. It was an epistemic crisis because he had assumed that values were driven by reason. That is to say, that the values of people arose from judgements made based empirically derived facts. Whenever better evidence was received from more empirical information, Du Bois felt that the level of humanity, or shared human values, would also rise commensurably. Also, if he produced work which clearly demonstrated that the problems which seemed endemic to Black people were really just problems which arose from the poverty most Black people experienced as a result of racism, then whites would agree with his results and work toward amicable and just solutions. It was an existential crisis for him because he could not just shrug his shoulders at the matter. Since his youth, he had always had a deep concern with the problems that affected "the other Black boys."[23] He had already committed to the work of his people. Now, Du Bois's realization that scientific evidence does not necessarily shape human values unless they serve their own self interests was demonstrative to him of the necessity and usefulness of the humanities in changing public opinion.

It was from this point forward that Du Bois's work would straddle the fence between science and a type of existential humanist philosophy invested in exposing the strange meaning of blackness during his lifetime. As a scientist, Du Bois wanted to use the tools of knowledge acquisition: observation, investigation, experimentation; to put forward facts from which truth claims would be a simple leap of logic. He now had grown to consider that the work the facts were allowed to perform in the consciousness, of the white people who were his intended audience, depended greatly on the perceptual framework in which they possessed. Through their perceptual framework, determinations about meaning and worth were made. This made it necessary for Du Bois to attempt to capture through verbal expression the incoherent space allotted to Black people. Du Bois's magnum opus, *Black Reconstruction*, was a clear example of this effort. In this text, Du Bois attempts to beat back the false representations of the actions of Black people, particularly Black politicians, during the period known as Reconstruction. Du Bois's world was a world where a nation could create the very conditions it knew would hinder the very human ability to flourish, and then create punishments for anyone who dared to rebel. Du Bois's world was also a world where Black people developed a unique ability to remain human and also thrive in spite of being starved, caged, and lynched, but Du Bois knew that the price extracted for such thriving might not be sustainable.

As an existential humanist philosopher, Du Bois placed humans, specifically Black people, at the center of his reflective activity, while seeking to demonstrate the humanity of the same and also shining a light on the immoral nature of the treatment they received from whites. This treatment was aimed toward dehumanizing and eliminating the means of creating a flourishing existence, seen here as akin to freedom by means of being freely able to develop. Du Bois wanted to use the tools of reason: logic, rhetoric, and imagination; to place within a frame the world of Black people with such clarity, that the previously mentioned leap of logic, required by Du Bois the scientist, would simply be a meeting of other intelligent minds, or a step instead of a leap. He would do this by also providing the tools, which could release persons from problematic perceptual frameworks. The very title of the book, *The Souls of Black Folk*, allowed Du Bois to set the stage for a different frame or reframing of the perception of Black people. To speak of Black people in terms of souls was to speak of them as human, and therefore beyond existing as mere brutes. Brutes are considered to be human in form, but not have human intellect. According to Aristotle in his *Nicomachean Ethics*, there are categories of humans that deserve to be slaves, and among these categories were those who are referred to as brutes.[24] Aristotle's ideas along with others were used to undergird the transatlantic slave trade, beginning in the Age of Enlightenment.

Du Bois's choice for a title of the book, *The Souls of Black Folk*, was an intentional act that cut right through to the very core of the "brute" concept which was also alluded to in Aristotle's book, *On the Soul*, Περι Ψυχης. This dialogue surrounding the fundamental nature of humanity was a great concern with many cords of contention from about the time of Plato and Aristotle during the Axial age until the European Renaissance. These various cords were braided into one approximation in the mind/body discussions. It was on this discussion that René Descartes would supply his thoughts through his *Discourse on Methods* when he made the declaration of the now-famous cogito, "I think therefore I am." The importance of this discussion as it pertains to Black people and my purpose for mentioning at this juncture is that if the use of the arguments by Aristotle, Descartes, and others for the purpose of segregating humanity in categories of brutes and intellectuals, could not be refuted then some portion of humanity Black people in particular, it could be argued, did not deserve the civil treatment afforded to those believed to have more intellect. As early as 1734, Anton Wilhelm Amo, a West African from Guinea (modern-day Ghana), recognized the importance of exposing contradiction in Descartes's work on the matter. Amo's dissertation was a refutation of Descartes's argument, and it was simultaneously an exposure of the European contradiction that this ability did not reside within the African. Thus, it was also a demonstration that a human being from West Africa, the very home of the Transatlantic Slave Trade could reason at the highest level of philosophical analysis and logical precision. In essence, Amo used reason at the highest level to expose two contradictions at once.

Du Bois's challenge in his book was to demonstrate that the humanity of Black people was not totally stripped away, as demonstrated by their spiritual strivings and also their creative imaginings as depicted in the sorrow songs. This was in spite of the tremendous efforts to dehumanize Black people, on the part of whites. It was answers such as this one provided by Du Bois to the challenges to Black people's humanity that gave rise to the modern era of the African American freedom struggle. The requirement for such a struggle was because the legal categorization of Negro as applied to Black people in America, a supposedly separate but equal status, was distinguished from being white in that it afforded to Black people only a meager and exploited existence. The ability under law for the guarantee of their rights as human to flourish was not seen as necessary. In part, this cavalier approach to the legal protection of Black people rested on the justifications provided by white scholars and was undergirded by the pseudoscience which began to be produced early in the Enlightenment.[25] Such a trend in thought could have this effect on one group of people only if they could be dehumanized ever so slightly, if they could be shown to possess a characteristic which indicated to others that human intelligence was not essential to their nature. This would mean that they had climbed only as far as three rungs from the top on the great chain of being, with God on the top rung and white people just below God. This would also mean that without the possession of this type of intellect, they were totally passive beings in terms of their affect on the world. Only humans with intellect can transform their dreams into reality in a manner that science refers to as human/environment interactions. This simply means that humans can change their environment to suit their needs and desires such that they can have or create a flourishing existence. In this sense, the pursuit of happiness, spoken of in the Declaration of Independence, is only possible for whites because only they have an intellect that allows for such a freedom. All others should be enslaved and thoroughly exploited. Hegel's juxtaposition of Africa as the dark continent creating nothing is in reference to these assumptions about Black people.[26]

In an attempt to recapture the earlier point about *Plessy v. Ferguson* and its influence on the development of the modern era of the African American freedom struggle, in terms of the maturation of American legal jurisprudence, *Plessy v. Ferguson* is emblematic of the intent found in the sentiment of Enlightenment philosophies, which remained forceful even after the demise of American chattel slavery. The effect of this intent can be understood through Du Bois's words:

> He began to have a dim feeling that, to attain his place in the world, he must be himself, and not another. For the first time he sought to analyze the burden he bore upon his back, that dead-weight of social degradation partially masked behind a half-named Negro problem. He felt his poverty; without a cent, without a home, without land, tools, or savings, he had entered into competition with rich, landed, skilled neighbors. To be a poor man is hard, but to be a poor race in a land of dollars is the very bottom of hardships. He felt the weight of his ignorance,—not simply of letters, but of life, of business, of the humanities; the accumulated sloth and shirking and awkwardness of decades and centuries shackled his hands and feet. Nor was his burden all poverty and ignorance. The red stain of bastardy, which two centuries of systematic legal defilement of Negro women had stamped upon his race, meant not only the loss of ancient African chastity, but also the hereditary weight of a mass of corruption from white adulterers, threatening almost the obliteration of the Negro home.[27]

In this passage, one can quickly recognize the absence of a free space for Black people to know and be themselves, whether this space is conceptual or material. This lack experienced by these Black people was intended to constrict and conscript their existence to a subservient class so that it might be argued that their existence was foreshadowed and preordained by God. It was a common notion in such august bodies as the British Royal Society, in which this very point was argued. It was also a regular portion of the white American Christian indoctrination.[28] As a matter of fact, this sentiment grounded Booker T. Washington's 1895 Atlanta Compromise, which played a major role in the comfort of the legislature in making the *Plessy v. Ferguson* decision. Although Washington did not believe Black people are preordained by God to be servants for whites, he was willing to accommodate the oppressive desires of whites. This was because he was under the impression that doing so would allow Black people to develop economic independence from whites without facing the violent reactions of whites to the incursion of Black people into white spaces. Unfortunately, Washington's accommodationist philosophy was flawed and shortsighted, for it took for granted that whites thought as a monolith. He didn't seem to realize that the violence Black people experienced was tied to class. Poor whites without political power used violence to control Black spaces. Also, he neglected to realize that it was not in the interest of wealthy whites and white politicians to serve as a buffer between poor whites and even the most accommodating Black people.

Attention upon the thought of African American philosopher Thomas Nelson Baker,[29] as portrayed in his 1903 dissertation, "The ethical significance of the connection between mind and body," is important to demonstrate that the problem arising from the writings of Aristotle, Descartes, and the pseudo-science and philosophies of the Enlightenment was understood to be central.[30] To be clear, Aristotle and Descartes were not making an argument to instigate the type of color-focused racism which ensued during the Enlightenment, but their arguments did lend themselves to such use. These writings were beginning to be confronted by others within the academy as well as in spaces exterior to the academy who sought to create correctives to the ideas that undergirded the oppressive forces which syllogistically sought to remove any philosophical premises that secured the legal status for the humanity of Black people. Such arguments as the one found in Baker's dissertation sought to remove the cover from any who would used the logic of the Enlightenment to absolve themselves of any malicious intent in terms of their racist actions. An example of such intent is found in the public remarks made by James K. Vardaman, the Democratic governor of Mississippi in 1907,

> How is the white man going to control the government? The way to do it is to pass laws to fit the white man and make the other people (Negroes) come to them. . . . If it is necessary every negro in the state will be lynched; it will be done to maintain white supremacy. . . . The XV Amendment ought to be wiped out. We all agree on that. Then why don't we do it?[31]

Baker seized upon the essential flaw found within the Cartesian framework, realizing that Descartes separated the human mind from the world. Although, Descartes's announced intent was to create a way of knowing based upon isolating only the things that could be known without doubt, he limited this way of knowing to the ability of ratiocination, only. In effect, this limitation also separated the mind from the body. The separation of the mind from the body is an impossible separation in the real world. If Descartes could not doubt that he was thinking then the realization that he was thinking of something should not have been doubted as well. Certainly, there were significant objects of his thoughts which could not be rightly doubted, also.

Baker while being thought of as an idealist was in reality a realist. This is easily seen in his notion that metaphysical thought begins with Being. Baker began his argument concerning the reality of the body by first asking the question, "Is the body, with its aches and pains, delights and pleasures, anything more than a fabrication of the mind?"[32] After posing the question, Baker then commits himself to a realist position, even though, to be fair, as an acknowledged Christian he would certainly have maintained some idealist commitments, also. After taking time to explain his notion of reality and purporting that it is akin to the meaning of being, Baker exposes the assertion in which his argument turns. This assertion is that being and action are inseparable.[33] "To be is to act, the inactive is the non-existent."[34] For Baker, there is no being without action and neither takes precedent. Baker refers to them as an indissoluble unity. The appearance of the two, we experience them in thoughts are as if one can be abstracted from the other, but in reality one implies the other. Being does not imply a specific action but it necessarily implies action. "That which does not act cannot be known."[35] When Descartes quipped that he knew that he was thinking, it implied that he was thinking of something and that he knew that he was thinking of something, which also subsequently meant, because there is no such thing as a disembodied thinker, Descartes was embodied in reality as he thought at a particular moment. So it was not just his thoughts that existed; his body participated in his existence, also.

It is after his explanation of the reality of the body that Baker set his aim on demonstrating the connection between the body and the mind. He begins with the portrayal of the body as containing the soul, which, accordingly, gives the body value. What Baker says of the body's value is the Kantian notion of, "It is the worth of the human soul that puts man in the realm of ends and forbids that he should ever be put in the realm of means." Baker describes this value by making a distinction between the body and soul, and the worth of the body without life or without the soul. For Baker, it is the body with the soul that clearly has the value, and this value is due largely because of the soul's ability to imagine. The soul can also act on this imagining. The argument for this value, stemming from this connection has importance here because of how Baker eventually equates the soul to the mind. According to Baker, when he uses the terms soul and the spirit he means what modern psychology refers to as the mind. This is akin to the earlier discussion concerning Du Bois's use of the term "soul."

Du Bois, was in many ways, the synthesis or focal point of the freedom movement, particularly the shift from the premodern to the modern. Du Bois shapes an ideal among African Americans of the scholar-activist. Before Du Bois there was none with the range of interests, writings, and activities, all aimed toward the same goal. Of course, there are many reasons for this, but the fact remains. One of the reasons has much to do with the dispute between Du Bois and Booker T. Washington. Many contingencies were connected to this debate, of which one example is what should be the predominant form of Black education, liberal arts or industrial training. Du Bois also brought a kind of systematic unity to this modern period that is only foreshadowed by others, but not completely present. Many names can be mentioned within this vein, such as Frederick Douglass, Martin Delany, David Walker, Alexander Crummell, and Ana Julia Cooper. However, all are missing at least one component, some more than one, that Du Bois mastered, of which today we take to be fundamental to a complete study of Black people. Most often, the range covered by Du Bois is expected today to be the production of many persons, if not an entire department. What the philosopher Ernst Cassirer says of Nicholas Cusanus could easily be applied to Du Bois in reference to the modern era of the African American freedom struggle.

> Any study that seeks to view the philosophy of the Renaissance as a systematic unity must take as its point of departure the doctrines of Nicholas Cusanus. Of all the philosophical movements and efforts of the Quattrocento, only his doctrines fulfill Hegel's demand; only they represent a "simple focal point" in which the most diverse rays are gathered. Cusanus is the only thinker of the period to look at all of the fundamental problems of his time from the point of view of one principle through which he masters them all.[36]

This one focal point for Du Bois, the problem of the color line, was a problem that produced a sequestered existence for those who were blacked by law and it was this created "blackness" that allowed others to view the problems which it produced as inherent pathologies.[37] Although the solution to the problem in the Modern Era could no longer come in the form of escape from a plantation, freedom continued to be thought of as possible and many continued to participate in freedom gazing.

Freedom Gazing

The legal status of Black people and their material existence, after the signing of the Thirteenth Amendment ending legal chattel slavery, continued to demonstrate the contradictions of American society. These contradictions produced both social and economic disparities between Black people and white people. Du Bois had this to say, "Meantime the immediate problem of the Negro was the question of securing existence of labor and income, of food and home, of spiritual independence and democratic control of the industrial process."[38] From this quote offered by Du Bois, an extrapolation might proceed such as, Black people had the legal status which declared their freedom, but no place to exact these freedoms and no protection existed of them of them as well. Basically, for Black people no place existed in which they could be free.

There are studies of Black people that are currently in print which show the subject matter to be complex and multifaceted. This current study does not intend to displace all previous studies. Its purpose is only to heed the call offered by Reed and in the performance of this task to offer a suggestion which can help better clarify the subject matter. This suggestion is that, to fully understand Black people during the modern era, the claim must at least in part be conditioned by an understanding of how the desire for freedom was driven by their material existence and how these two components shaped the culture of Black people. In order to extend further the claim of freedom gazing existing as a major driver of Black culture, it must be shown that Black people had a reasonable conception of freedom and the possibility of its actualization. It must also be shown that the thread of freedom gazing remains throughout the modern era and is pervasive on some level. No reasonably intelligent person would argue that there was not a significant desire for freedom among Black people enslaved in America prior to 1865 or that this desire was not a driving force of their cultural developments. However, there might exist those who would raise questions about the continuity, pervasiveness, or the duration of this influence throughout the modern era. In the next two brief sections, the aim consists in rationally extinguishing these concerns while also demonstrating the significance of the freedom gaze as a means analysis and interpretation.[39]

As with the previous section of this chapter, in this section we center the writings of W. E. B. Du Bois as a means of casting light upon freedom gazing.[40] From Du Bois, the discussion will expand throughout the entirety of the book to demonstrate continuity and pervasiveness of the concept. To begin with, if one willingly accepts that Du Bois's synthesizes the previous generations' concern for blackness and freedom, then one might equally accept that there exists a chiastic structure that extends beyond Du Bois, in which a Du Boisian type of syntheses of ideas is perpetuated. This assertion must of course be demonstrated, but first finding the notion plausible does help to begin this transition. For example, in *The Souls of Black Folk*, Du Bois wrote, "few men ever worshipped freedom with half such unquestioning faith as did the American Negro for two centuries."[41] This statement is offered as a type of substantive expression that depicts the notion of Black people as freedom gazers. It is quite clear through this statement that Du Bois's intended meaning is to describe those of the generations which preceded him; however, what is not evident is whether Du Bois also believes freedom is possible and that he continued the tradition of freedom gazing. What may account for the dissimilarity is Du Bois's moment of existence which occurred under different material conditions than those before him. Du Bois is not stating that he no longer finds the goal of freedom or the struggle for freedom meaningful, quite the contrary. His intent is filtered through the contemporaneity of his moment and his awareness of the nearly successful attempts by whites to deflate the desires of Black people. In accordance with the aim of this section, the universal nature of this claim by Du Bois written in 1903, is offered as a demonstration of his attempt to show that the desire for freedom, at least until his existence, shaped the perceptual framework of Black people in a manner that was consistent, pervasive, and had endured for a tremendously long period.

Du Bois was a freedom gazer. Using a type of loose logical structure and a rather laymen's method toward definition and categorization, this statement could stand alone, unchallenged in everyday conversation. But, in order to show Du Bois as a freedom gazer while withstanding challenges from those who have a vested interest in knowing and writing practically every description possible concerning Du Bois, will require just a bit more effort in terms of reasoning. This aim does not require finding some reference where Du Bois uses the label freedom gazer in reference to himself. That type of occurrence alone would not resolve the issue. If a reference such as this were to be found, I would also need an accompanying definition, in addition to this type of reference. However, after a thorough amount of adequate research, I suspect there exists no such exact reference in which Du Bois uses this nomenclature. Besides, if such a reference existed, then I suspect the announcement of its discovery would have already taken place. In order to make this type of label a lasting one, first there must be clarity about the type of activity being performed. In others words, is this the creation of a novel theoretical conception, complete with neologisms, which is being mapped onto Du Bois. The type of theoretical conception being referred to here is the type of universal claim with its own internal logic that is general enough such as to be sufficient in many types of human activity. Or, is this the identification of a specific occurrence relative to the Black people identified by the parameters previously mentioned such that its occurrence, despite being unnamed, has sufficient frequency and once named it exists as a piece to a puzzle, which required only to have its occurrence to be separated from other occurring activity for recognition. The latter of these activities is what is intended in this writing. Its ability to be universalized is not to be denied; however, the universalization of such is only in reference to specific human activity that occurs universally because of the presence of similar conditions such as oppression along with segregation. Hitler's Germany and South African Apartheid are two contemporary examples.

Many statements and actions from Du Bois's long career could be put forward as useful in this effort; however, his words of reflections, particularly those from the three ethnographies establish a more emphatic depiction than does the activity of building a case from works interpreted as such without having his explicit acknowledgment that this was his intent. *Dusk of Dawn* serves as an excellent choice for this exhibition, because of the late timing of its publication in Du Bois's life and his intended purpose of painting himself as one who was integrally involved in the struggle for freedom while having worked out some comparable solution. Du Bois began the text with an "Apology," meaning a defense, as used here, of his lifelong chosen activity. In this defense, he says this of his written intent,

> I have written then what is meant to be not so much my autobiography as the autobiography of a concept of a race, elucidated, magnified and doubtless distorted in the thoughts and deeds which were mine. If the first two books were written in tears and blood, this is set down no less determinedly but yet with wide hope in some more benign fluid. Wherefore I have hesitated in call it *Dusk of Dawn*.[42]

One might ask, did not Du Bois see himself as free? To this Du Bois answered,

> I was by long education and continual compulsion and daily reminder, a colored man in a white world; and that white world often existed primarily, so far as I was concerned, to see with sleepless vigilance that I kept within bounds. All this made me limited in physical movement and provincial in thought and dream. I could not stir, I could not act, I could not live without taking into careful daily account the reaction of my white environing world.[43]

Another question one might ask is could Du Bois or some other similarly situated person within the modern era act outside the purview the freedom aesthetic. In other words, can human beings act outside their particular moment in time and without accordance to their aesthetic experience, making no judgements in response. To be human is to exist and to make some judgements according our aesthetic experience or sensory perception. But, it seems that this might be partially be possible in terms of our conscious rational decisions; however, the purpose of reason as I see is to facilitate the act of living.[44] To act without any accord to one's moment in time would be out of line with this facilitation, unless doing so is proven to be harmful, in which case better methods should be attempted. However, attempting better methods is still to act within accordance to one's moment. The previous quote from Du Bois speaks to this possibility generally, but a more specific answer relates back to the earlier discussion concerning experiential moments which shape our perceptual frameworks by providing the signs and symbols which bound our existential judgments. In this sense, the freedom aesthetic becomes as much apart of our overall perceptual framework as does national culture or family traditions. These can also be jettisoned, but this jettisoning requires conscious effort. And, there is always the ever-looming question of why.

ETHNIC REFLECTIVE CANON

The ethnic reflective canon is probably the most significant and conspicuously revealing factor of the freedom gaze in the modern era. Black people who expanded this ethnic reflective canon, during the modern era, did so through the freedom gaze. Du Bois, as a freedom gazer, was instrumental in affecting a shift in the canon, but he did not singularly initiate the canon.[45] If the origin of the canon was located through its earliest components, the unwritten lines of the "black and unknown bards" spoken of by James Weldon Johnson would certainly be among the number. The function of the canon in the real lives of Black folk, in terms of expanding the conception of blackness beyond the usual disparaging remarks and exposing their lived experience, provides a frame for deciding what pieces should be considered in terms of priority. However, as the shift from Black enslavement by rule and law moved toward a Black theoretical freedom limited by the legal or political power to actualize this freedom; a shift in the methods occurred that Black people used to create the concrete actualization of their freedom where only the theoretical abstractions were present. In doing so, many Black thinkers realized that this concreteness needed to first be conceived in the intellect and this would require the captivation of the minds and souls of Blacks and whites through written ideas. Even before the ending of slavery, there are examples such as David Walker's "Appeal." But, whatever the scheme used here for the choice of the first work for assessment, someone would always be of the opinion that some text other than the one chosen should be included first. For this reason, Ida B. Wells's writings, particularly *Southern Horrors: Lynch Law in all Phases* and *A Red Record,* cannot be surpassed except only by preference. The purpose for choosing a book to map in this section is to establish a measure for the book and the author's role in the canon and their importance to the community's freedom struggle overall. This measure will not be a determinant of the ranking of the book during the time period of circulation. That would require a much longer list than intended to be included.

This measure is only meant to show that such a canon existed, the purpose of such a canon, and to assess the author in terms of their aim of community development and social transformation within the struggle.

After slavery, the Southern capitalist and politicians continued to desire to use violence to guarantee the ability to exploit Blacks in America. Violence was used to thwart the vote, to limit travel, and to control the ability to earn a living. Basically, violence barred Black people from humanistically flourishing. Ida B. Wells recognized how violence was being used most prevalently through lynching, and she directed the full effort of her intellectual energy in a frontal attack this crime against humanity. Although, her entrance into activism was in a lawsuit over being denied the ability to ride in the car of her choice on a train, a lawsuit which she eventually lost, she soon turned her attention to lynchings when her good friend Thomas Moore was hanged in the city of Memphis. Her chosen method of activism pertaining to lynchings was through investigative journalism and sociological documentation.

In 1892, Wells composed a small pamphlet entitled *Southern Horrors: Lynch Law in all Phases*. This work epitomizes the journalistic style she utilized much of the time, which included a type of sociological descriptive method making use of numerical data to expose the true facts surrounding lynchings. In 1895, she composed *A Red Record: Tabulated Statistics and Alleged Causes of Lynchings in the United States 1892–1893–1894,* in which she documented lynching statistics over a three-year period. Her efforts were praised by Frederick Douglass for the bravery displayed in terms of her willingness to be truthful in spite of the threat of death. These works pushed for reformation and justice but were not radical in nature. By radical, it is meant here that she is not calling for a major change to the American system of government. She wants the current system to work more justly and that white citizens display an equitable moral attitude in terms of their treatment of their fellow citizens. Although, to be fair she does display glimpses of a proto-Ethiopic[46] thought.

In relationship to the freedom gaze, what is significant in Wells's writings is recognition of the need for community development and social transformation. Her activism is linked and could be said to be her publishings, much the same as Du Bois was a scholar-activist. Another person who prefigures Du Bois is the renowned educator Anna Julia Cooper, who believed just as Du Bois that education was the key to a better more democratic future. In fact it seems that if one were to read the work of Anna Julia Cooper alongside that of Ida B. Wells, there is a definite genetic thread that leads directly to Du Bois's work.[47] Wells's work clearly demonstrates a desire for a particular vision of freedom that is tied to a thriving Black community. What shapes and gives credibility to the existence of the modern era of the African American freedom struggle is the social network that developed, which becomes visible as we view the contact between these three and others. These three provide a glimpse into what social scientists and social network analysts refer to as a sociocentric network. Simply put, socio-centric networks are enclosed by boundaries and are also known as a "network in a box."[48]

The triad was utilized as the structural foundation to build the text around and to demonstrate the reality of the modern era of the African American freedom struggle because it is said to be the basic building block of a society. This idea can be traced to Georg Simmel's conception of "associations of three."[49] The notion that the triad forms a stronger network than the dyad, and is also the basic building block of a social network, stems from its ability to accommodate discord. With the dyad, there exists an all-or-nothing element when disagreements arise. However, in the triad there exists absorb disputes. Beyond the intricacies that distinguish the dyad and the triad, the importance of the African American social network which was formed informally during slavery and took on a new dynamic during the modern era is that is likely that Black Americans would not have survived without it. The survival of humans in general is dependent upon social networks, particularly as children. Without a social network, we possess extreme vulnerability that hinders our survival elements and a lack of ability in accomplishing important tasks. One of these important tasks is self-defense which is accomplished by a number methods. Many of the human methods for performing self defense rely upon intellection. It is the method of intellection, which shapes the aspect of the African American social network, also known as the Black community, being focused upon in this text as we explore the modern era of the African American freedom struggle. Many write about the social connections Du Bois had with other thinkers exterior to the Black community of his day, but it was the connections with the Black people that were striving for freedom in the oppressive structure that is America and around the world that he formed his most significant ties. He clearly recognized the salvific function this network held in terms of the survival of Black people during the modern era. This is where he saw the aim of his work and these are the people who read his work and took it seriously during his lifetime. These three form the first triad of the social network in my simulation of how the social network of the modern era might look.

MOVEMENT MAP

As stated in the previous chapter, "Mapping the Movement," which this section is also labeled, points to an attempt to acknowledge the correlation between the concept of movement and the temporospatial reality of movement. Maps are used to determine location and spatial relationships at a given point in time. Here, the idea of "mapping the movement" is meant to perform a similar function in terms of the movement. The reference points that will be utilized to make determinations concerning these temporospatial relationships will be the predominating ideas: peace, rebellion, revolution, and freedom. In terms of plotting, and in order to find a location on a map, there are two tools of which will be required: coordinates and scales. For the purpose of locating an individual in terms of the freedom movement geography, I will make use of the following categories as coordinating tools: speeches/talks, action/activity, writings. For the purpose of scalar quantities in terms of the coordinating categories, this analysis will use the individual's commitment to the concept, in place of numerical value, to measure their temporospatial relationship to the notion of freedom. The individual's commitment to freedom might well be verbalized and written about but they might also subscribe to the notion of peace at all cost. Their subscription to peace will put them in a position of sacrificing freedom for the sake of peace, therefore the correlation between the desire for peace and their commitment to freedom produces a low position in terms of their movement participation. No number is needed to represent this contradiction in their commitment.

The following chart is offered as a visual representation of just how such a mapping of ideas can be visualized. This chart presents the relationship of the thinker to concepts of peace, rebellion, revolution, and freedom are explored in chapter 1. Based upon the information as displayed, Cooper ranks the lowest on the scale in relation to actions that will produce freedom. On the other hand, Du Bois ranks the highest in terms of his relationship to freedom on the humanistic expression scale, but Wells and Du Bois rank equal in their relationship to freedom on the Community Development and Social Transformation scale. In the following chapters, only the chart will be shown without the accompanying in depth explanation.

{D= W. E. B. Du Bois; W= Ida B. Wells; C= Anna Julia Cooper}

Table 2.1: A Chart of the Ideas of the Freedom Movement——> Cooper, Du Bois, and Wells

	CD/ST	Humanistic Expression
Freedom		
Revolution		D
Rebellion	W, D	W
Peace	C	C

NOTES

1. Anthony Sean Neal, "New Directions for the Study of King and Thurman," *The Acorn: Philosophical Studies in Pacifism and Nonviolence,* 20, no. 1.
2. The logic for the development of such a notion can be found in Alfred North Whitehead's explanation of actual occasion; John Dewey's notion of lived experience; and even Bergson notion of duration. There certainly others who offer rich descriptions of the concept being put forward such as: Heidegger, Gilson, and Bernard Lonergan; however, the description being offered here is an attempt to account for the interplay between sensory perception of experience detected empirically and the act knowing or understanding through a process of identification and assessment through reason. Certainly, I don't want to imply that all the thinkers listed agree; mentioning them in this fashion is simply to point out that the relevance and even necessary nature of asking such a question.
3. René Descartes, Tom Griffith, and John Veitch. *Discourse on Method: Meditations on the First Philosophy; The Principles of Philosophy* (New York: Barnes & Noble, 2004), p. 88.
4. Edward L. Smith, *Prehension: A Process Version of Friedrich Schleiermacher's Theory of the Feeling of Absolute Dependence of God* (Ann Arbor: UMI Dissertation Services, 1998), p. 117.
5. Anthony Sean Neal, *Common Ground: A Comparison of the Ideas of Consciousness in the Writings of Howard W. Thurman and Huey P. Newton* (Trenton: Africa World Press), p. 27.
6. In its current acceptance, the term "phantasm" signifies a representation or apparition distinct from the ordinary reality of things and frequently subjective in character. thomas aquinas define phantasm functionally as a likeness of a particular thing (Summa theologiae 1a, 84.7 ad 2). In Platonic philosophy, objective reality as perceived and distorted by the five senses. . . . Something seen but having no physical reality; a phantom or apparition.
7. Persisting ideas are ideas communicated or learned through experienced.
8. Colors, shapes, sizes, etc.
9. Anthony Sean Neal. *Common Ground: A Comparison of the Ideas of Consciousness in the Writings of Howard W. Thurman and Huey P. Newton* (Trenton: Africa World Press, 2015).
10. W. E. B. Du Bois, "Science and Empire," *Dusk of Dawn,* LOA edition, p. 603.
11. Ibid.
12. April 23, 1899.
13. P. 363, *Souls of Black Folk*, LOA edition.
14. Freedom gazer—in simple terms, one constantly searching for freedom and also takes freedom to be a real possibility in some reasonable iteration, while admitting that freedom is not their current condition. In reference to this book and in accordance with the first chapter, a freedom gazer acts in relationship to a perceptual framework which developed because of the experience of oppression in America. It shaped the thoughts, writings, and activities of Black people during the modern era. Certain markers were developed based upon disposition toward discovered during the

research of the modern era. As discussed in chapter 1, the dispositions will be used as markers in a type of continuum to discuss the participant's activity in the freedom struggle and their activity in terms of commitment to the struggle for freedom. This commitment is assessed in relationship to revolution, rebellion, and peace. These markers of the participant's commitment to the freedom struggle can be used to also chart the commitment. The chart will be discussed in a later section in this chapter.

15. Du Bois, *Dusk of Dawn*, LOA, p. 557.

16. *The Souls of Black Folk*, *Darkwater*, and *Dusk of Dawn*.

17. Du Bois, *Dusk of Dawn*, LOA, p. 551.

18. See Du Bois, *Dusk of Dawn*, LOA, p. 602; Ida B. Wells, *The Light of Truth* (New York: Penguin), p. 314.

19. Edward Allen Jones. *Voices of Négritude: the Expression of Black Experience in the Poetry of Senghor, Césaire & Damas* (Valley Forge, PA: Judson Press), pp. 15–17.

20. L. D. Keita. *Philosophy and African Development Theory and Practice* (Dakar, Senegal: CODESRIA, 2011), p. 37.

21. At the beginning of the modern era of the African American freedom movement, a shift in the legal status of Black people in America occurred, predicated by the decision of the *Plessy v. Ferguson* Supreme Court trial, which defined in legal the definitional upon which blackness was to be understood. William James Hull Hoffer, *Plessy v. Ferguson: Race and Inequality in Jim Crow America.* (Lawrence: University Press of Kansas), pp. 1–8.

22. This point is meant to create a contradistinction, but not to be taken contrary, with Anthony Appiah's "The Uncomplete Argument." In Appiah's article he states that, "Throughout his life, Du Bois was concerned not just with the meaning of race but with the truth about it." Appiah's contention with Du Bois hinges upon whether Du Bois's notion concerning race was, in fact, the truth about race. This is important when considering that according to Appiah, Du Bois was mistaken in his conception of race which relied upon a socio-historical conception and not a biological or anthropological conception. The space that I wish to create between Appiah and myself rests upon my view of what exactly was the object Du Bois's highest concern. I take this object to be the value of the truth being put forward in conjunction with truth itself and not truth alone. To my point, I put forward this quote from *Dusk of Dawn*, in which Du Bois describes an event that took place on April 23, 1899. (The year is important because of the advanced nature the event occurs in Du Bois's life.) "Two considerations thereafter broke in upon my work and eventually disrupted it: first, one not be a calm, cool, and detached scientist while Negroes were lynched, murdered, and starved; and secondly, there was no such definite demand for the scientific work of the sort that I was doing, as I had confidently assumed would be easily forthcoming." So to Appiah's point, Du Bois did see the dawn coming, but was not allowed to focus upon the sun, being hindered by the way in which the social and legal conceptions of race operated in his world. Anthony Appiah, "The Uncomplete Argument: Du Bois and the Illusion Race," Critical Inquiry, 12, no. 1, pp. 21–37; Nathan Huggins, ed., *W. E. B. Du Bois' Writings* (New York: The Library of America, 1995), p. 603.

23. Du Bois, *Souls*, LOA edition, p. 364.

24. Aristotle, *Nicomachean Ethics*, Book VII; (Aristotle's thoughts on brutes is consistent in other works) *The Politics*, Book I; and *On the Soul*, Book III.

25. , Emmanuel Chukwudi Eze. *Race and the Enlightenment: A Reader* (Malden, MA: Blackwell, 1997), pp. 1–10.

26. Hegel, *Philosophy of History* (Mineola, NY: Dover Publications, 1956), p. 99.

27. Du Bois, *Souls,* LOA edition, p. 368.

28. Adolph Reed, and Kenneth W. Warren, *Renewing Black Intellectual History The Ideological and Material Foundations of African American Thought* (New York: Routledge, 2010), pp. 98–105.

29. Baker was the first African American person to get a P.hD. in philosophy. John H. McClendon, III and Stephen C. Ferguson, II, *African American Philosophers and Philosophy* (London: Bloomsbury, 2019), p. 44.

30. Thomas Nelson Baker, "The Ethical Significance of the Connection between Mind and Body" (PhD Dissertation, Yale 1903), title page.

31. Robert Brisbane, *The Black Vanguard*, p. 25.

32. Thomas Nelson Baker, "The Ethical Significance of the Connection between Mind and Body" (PhD Dissertation, Yale 1903), pp. 96–103.

33. Ibid., p. 16.

34. Ibid.

35. Ibid, p. 17.

36. Ernst Cassirer, *The Individual and the Cosmos* (Brooklyn: Angelico Press, 1968), p. 7.

37. Nahum Dimitri Chandler, *X—the Problem of the Negro As a Problem for Thought* (New York: Fordham, 2014), pp. 12–15.

38. Du Bois, *Dusk of Dawn*, p. 557.

39. By analysis, it is meant mean approaching logical concerns; and by interpretation, it is meant approaching epistemic concerns.

40. For the full exposure of the concept, refer to chapter 1.

41. Du Bois, *The Souls of Black Folk*, p. 366.

42. Ibid., p. 552.

43. Ibid., p. 653.

44. Alfred North Whitehead also says that reason allows humans to fulfill the aim of our final cause; which is to live, live well, live better. Alfred North Whitehead, *The Function of Reason* (Boston: Beacon, 1971), p. 8.

45. Adolph Reed and Kenneth W. Warren, *Renewing Black Intellectual History The Ideological and Material Foundations of African American Thought* (New York: Routledge, 2015), pp. 252–262.

46. Proto-ethiopic is a "back to Africa" tendency which preceded Marcus Garvey.

47. Joy James, "The Profeminist Politics of W. E. B. Du Bois—with Respects to Anna Julia Cooper and Ida B. Wells Barnett," *The Thought of W. E. B. Du Bois*, Bernard Bell, James Stewart, Emily Grosholz, eds. (New York: Routledge, 1996).

48. Charles Kadushin, *Understanding Social Networks: Theories, Concepts and Findings* (Oxford: Oxford, 2018), p. 17.

49. Georg Simmel, and Kurt H. Wolff, *The Sociology of Georg Simmel* (New York: Free Press, 1964), pp. 135–136.

Chapter 3

From Harlem to Paris (And Back)

VALUE AS FREEDOM IN BLACK HUMANITY

In the first chapter, essential questions were provided that have helped to facilitate reflections and to formulate the frame through which humanity, in this study, is understood. This study should be understood foremost to be a humanistic one. Once that is sufficiently understood, then its importance is found in the central theoretical principle, which is "humanness" is not a biologically given state; it is rather created in culture. Much of what humans know and hence, what drives their practice are historical and cultural constructs. African American culture, in the modern era, was formed in the midst of a struggle for freedom and from which developed a culturally constructed notion of freedom. The existential crisis of struggling for freedom produced a people but not a single people type. Also, the diversity of human types created was not a static creation. It must be remembered that being human is an ever-evolving and changing knowledge state. Like all such constructs, it must be created and, once created, constantly refined and articulated. Some parts of it must be refuted and abandoned. All of it requires being disseminated, transmitted, and taught. All cultures include groups of people whose central role is to maintain or enhance the human status of the people. These are groups of people largely consist of artists, philosophers, historians, poets, and other intellectuals. In short, these are the people who take the human being as their subject of study and creation. These artists, philosophers, historians, poets, and other intellectuals engage in the "heavy lifting" of creating, writing, and managing the social institutions that present human achievements to the whole community.

Similar to the last chapter, which ended with the social network triad of Cooper, Wells, and Du Bois; and so it is that this chapter will begin with the examination of the social network triad of Hubert Harrison, William H. Ferris, and Alain Locke. There will be comparisons of their writings, and the social transformations they intended to create. Although this study may appear to be linear in nature, because of the nature that books naturally emit, which might seem to imply causation, it is not intended to be an all-inclusive list of the figures who participated in the freedom struggle nor those who appear to fit the model. Figures included in this study are those whose (intended) transformation was significant enough to be interpreted as international even during their day. These figures created writings as well as performed social actions; and more notably, their actions have been significantly documented. The fundamental premises of their arguments will be put forth to demonstrate an interrelatedness. A major focus of this chapter is the idea of the value of personhood.

Struggling for freedom,[1] freedom gazing, and contributing to the ethnic reflective canon should at this point be considered, especially where this text is concerned, meaningful with respect to the freedom movement. As it concerns struggling for freedom in today's terms, people sometimes use this phrase to mean passively enduring instead of actively struggling by some practical means. In my first book, the practical means of actively struggling focused upon was community development efforts in whatever fashion. One of the proponents, Huey P. Newton, discussed in that book cofounded a revolutionary-minded political party, and the other proponent, Howard W. Thurman, cofounded a religious community. Each proponent intended their actions to be a turn from old ways of thinking, while also rupturing the previous way of relating to the outer community. The development of community set the groundwork for the possibility of a social transformation occurring. People coming together in this manner become cognizant of shared concerns while realizing their potential as a community. Many different community development efforts such as these occurred during the modern era. Their aim was social transformation or freedom.

One such effort in community development was the American Negro Academy founded by Alexander Crummell. Admittedly, a critique that might be leveled against the mentioning of this organization is that it represented the thoughts of an elite few who formed the Black intelligentsia. However, the relevance of this organization does not commence with the members' intent, but it begins with the scope of the organization. In order to fully grasp the complexity of the moment that produced this organization and may even have provided the catalyst for its elitist proclivity, there must be an investigation into major events culpable in compelling Crummell to see its necessity, while also throwing light on Crummell's and others disposition toward these events. These events are the death of Crummell (1898), the *Plessy v. Ferguson* decision (1896), and the speech known as the "Atlanta Compromise" (1895), given by Booker T. Washington at the Atlanta Cotton Exposition.[2] Of course, there are any number of ancillary events that occurred in the particular lives of the individual founders; however, the events listed were mentioned enough in the writings of the main proponents and others, that it would be easy to argue that these events also serve as experiential moments in the becoming of Black people, themselves.

By far, if someone were to ask me which of these three events was the most significant, I would respond by saying, "Why *Plessy*, of course!" However, that response probably is a symptom of my historical deformation or presentism. In fact, from my research on this particular moment in history, it is quite difficult to determine which event had the greater impact on these leaders such that they would found an organization with the characteristics of the American Negro Academy. One can only suspect and my suspicions lead me to conclude that it was not the *Plessy* verdict, but instead it was Washington's Atlanta Compromise. There are several clues that portend to this being the correct position for which to argue. The most obvious is that segregation in some form was already in effect before the adjudication of the *Plessy* verdict. Actually, it was the existence of the phenomenon of segregation which caused Black people to seek redress within the courts. Immediately following the Civil War, the passage of the Thirteenth through Fifteenth amendments were ratified with the aim of securing the freedom of Black people, but white backlash, in the form of the Ku Klux Klan and Black Codes, became also more visible.

Although the segregationist acts and behaviors were pervasive, the aim was really focused on discouraging Black people from voting. By all accounts, these actions were successful in decreasing Black people's voting strength as evidenced by the steep decline in Black elected officials. They also contributed to the mass migration of Black people to the North in what is referred to as the first migration. So then, one question that arises is, if these acts were successful, why did the speech by Booker T. Washington have its specific effect on Black leadership? In other words, there were many atrocities regularly occurring that certainly had deep effects on the material conditions of Black life. This much is historically acknowledged by the implementation of the Klan Act of 1871 by the then President Grant who deemed the organization to be terroristic in nature.[3] Lynching became a tool to decrease Black voter turnout. There was also the removal of Federal troops from the South by President Rutherford B. Hayes as a condition of the Hayes/Tilden Compromise of 1877, which again exposed Black people to the unrestrained terroristic threat of white violence. So why, then, was Washington's speech seen as an existential threat and the cause of profound consternation such that it has remained a point of reference or an inflection point in Black understanding of the Black self becoming in the American Moment even until the present day?

In order to heal an issue of this type within a text such as this one, that takes as its aim to provide a reframing of a period, but only a frame without all of the intricacies of the full picture, the framing or boundary must provide a clear view of the author's perspective. Therefore, in keeping with this limitation, it becomes fundamental to restate the framing notion of the entire text. This book is about the struggle for freedom of Black people in America. So then the question becomes whether Washington was a participant in the struggle. The answer to this question will also throw light on the previous question, why was Washington viewed as an existential threat by certain individuals in the movement? A fundamental commitment of those who participated in the freedom struggle, particularly those who formed the core of its educated elite, was to their declaration of humanity and as such, this commitment also extended to their desire for equal treatment under the law. For many, this move was tied to their religious conviction. They were children of God and could share in the same rewards that all other children of God enjoyed. For others, it was a simple claim of logical construction formed with syllogistic clarity. In order to escape contradiction, "all men [humans] are created equal," simply meant and must at all times mean all men [humans], or otherwise put, what applied to some applied to all. In the twenty-first century iteration of the United States, equal justice of under the law has become embedded into the cultural genetics, even if not yet equally enforced, but the Black people of Washington's day were demanding something that had not yet become conceptualized by all.

Also, extending necessarily from this claim is the notion that if the claim does not hold, then the minimum value of having at least the right to life does not exist. And, if there is no right to life, by further extension, there is no right to liberty or the pursuit of happiness. This certainly includes conceptually that whatever is understood to be attributed to the possibility of a flourishing life, Black people had no right to that. It is the importance of this last point that Washington seemed to have misapprehended or failed to consider altogether, even though he considered himself and was considered to be struggling for freedom. However, others like Crummell understood this point clearly. Washington was of the belief that there existed a practical inequality based upon the notion that Black people had not labored enough to partake of full citizenship.[4] Alexander Crummell's sentiments on the matter were as follows,

> One would suppose from the universal demand for the mere industrialism for this race of ours, that the Negro had been going daily to dinner parties, eating terrapin and indulging in champagne; and returning home at night, sleeping on beds of eiderdown; breakfasting in the morning bed, and then having his valet to clothe him daily in purple just now, the American people, tired of all this Negro luxury, was calling to supply his needs by sweatful toil in the cotton fields.[5]

For Alexander Crummell, along with W. E. B. Du Bois, Monroe Trotter, and others, Washington's words on September 18, 1895, were unacceptable. Crummell's reaction to Washington's accommodating virtue was to establish the American Negro Academy in 1897.[6] The ANA was established as an elite society of scholarly individuals who presented papers for the purpose of providing commentary, criticism and ideas about race, culture, and the future of Black people in American society. Papers presented ranged from Crummell's "Civilization, the Primal Need of the Race,"[7] and Du Bois's "The Conservatism of Race Traits, and Tendencies of the Negro,"[8] to an invited paper delivered in 1920 by Robert T. Browne on "Einstein's Theory of Relativity."[9] One question that could be asked of Crummell's action is why did he feel that his response was adequate? Or, in other words was his response an equal and or greater than reaction? What was the exact existential threat created by Washington to which Crummell was responding? As stated earlier, Washington discounted the very humanity of Black people. To put this another way, along with the connection that Washington created referring to Black people as a source of labor for white people and nothing more, he consequently attached to Black people the status of servants for white people as a purpose. In doing so, Washington dislodged, from Black people, the ability to choose their own purpose or options. This essentially devalued Black life by creating a life cycle with little possibility of flourishing.

Crummell based his ideas about the ANA upon the fundamental claim that civilization was a primal need, and as such, it provided the spiritual and idealistic alternative to all whose primary concern was material wealth.[10] Uplift, progress, or an upward aim, for Crummell was a natural phenomena for humans when unhindered by such things as race-based oppression. For Crummell, uplift was a notion that was stitched into a grand conception of being. Crummell was thoroughly an idealist, and as an idealist, he had this to say, "The Negro problem in the U.S. is a problem of ideas. There is a present, but fleeting movement, to give it the respect of materialism; but they who are making this endeavor, will be just as successful as they would be who should attempt to turn the needle to the Equator, instead of to the pole."[11] Crummell's idealism was by no means ironic. While at Cambridge, he had been a student of the Cambridge Platonist William Whewell.[12] It was there that he developed the view that to do philosophy or the life of the mind more generally, in terms of the exchange of ideas, is the highest form of life. He would have probably agreed in part with Rene Descartes that humans were the res cogitans, the thinking thing. This has import owing to the stress and value placed on mental activity in relation to other actions humans perform. It is not clear what value, if any, Crummell would attach to nonmental activity or how far he would have distanced it from mental activity. However, as Crummell saw it, Black people demonstrated this ability in terms of artistic creation, critical assessment, moral critiques, and rational attempts at problem solving. Therefore, in its scope, the ANA was uniquely aimed at performing all of these actions to offset the Washingtonian accommodationist philosophy, while also restoring value to Black minds. And, at least for Crummell, it seems that this was far more important than the value Black people accrued through their labor, regardless of whether white people realized this value or not. Black people were ends, not means.

VALUE AS A PROBLEM OF THOUGHT

The substantiation and acknowledgment of the life of the mind, among Black people, was deemed to have value because of its ability to make the individual free. This is the impetus Crummell had in insisting upon the importance of a liberal arts education. However, the response to Crummell's ideological call was variegated. For example, initially Du Bois's ideas on the matter mirrored Crummell's. In Washington, D.C., Du Bois once suggested to high school graduates, "that they would do well to model their lives on St. Francis of Assisi, who renounced wealth and status for a life of service and hardship."[13] While on faculty at Atlanta University, Du Bois felt that Mammonism[14] exchanges the value of being human, found in a liberal arts education that gives one the information to maintain freedom, for what is seen as quick money. Obviously, Crummell and Du Bois, among others, placed emphasis on the actualizing of the life of the mind through intellectual performance in intellectual spaces.[15] A different type of response to Crummell's ideological call, one made by Howard University Philosopher professor Alain Locke, was to think about how one might think about the problem of the color line and how it unfolds as a problem of the value of the culture of a marginalized group. In other words, Locke was concerned with the metacognitive act while examining the nature of value and culture along with their relationship to race. Therefore, Locke saw the problem of blackness, which Du Bois tried to define phenomenologically, as a problem of the value of Black culture. His undertaking of this question actually undergirds the ongoing New Negro move that was happening in Black culture, and is categorically a different question than either Crummell or Du Bois attempted at that point.[16]

As early as 1915, Locke's thoughts on race was to define it as a social construction. Leonard Harris wrote in *The Journal of Ethics*, "Although the theoretical basis for the idea of races as social constructions was initially presented in his 1915–1916 lecture series, its development continued even in the face of employment insecurity."[17] According to Harris, Locke continued to express his ideas of race relations in his many writings but didn't write his first extended philosophical piece on the matter until 1935, which was titled, "Value and Imperatives."[18] In the 1915–1916 lecture series, Locke wrote,

> The sense of race really antedates anything in its name, in the etymology of it, because just as long as you have groups of people knit together by a kinship feeling and who realize that different practices operate in their society from those which operate in other societies and therefore determine their treatment of other groups, then you really have what is the germ of race sense.[19]

However, the statement was not published until 1992 by Jeffrey C. Stewart. For Locke, whatever racial inequalities existed and led some to think that certain groups had less value, these should instead look to historical causes. Even prejudices toward color, for Locke, could be seen as created tensions from the desire for power by elites.[20]

In the 1928 article of Locke, "The Contribution of Race to Culture," Locke locates himself on the subject of civilization while relating the subject of social race[21] to culture.[22] He begins the article by affirming that race is essential to culture, so that he can inquire about the possibility of the existence of cultural differences coinciding with race differences. This conditional hinges on whether the available historical evidence concerning this matter is correct. However, Locke disrupts any possibility of a gesture toward a negative response by stipulating that even when we think it is impossible, it is more than likely owing to the fact that all cultures are prone to dismiss the notion that they are developments of cultural appropriation and mosaic developments. Considering the nature of thought as it pertains to value in relationship to race forces all who participate in this type of thought activity to first come to the realization that they may hold some notions to be universal when they should be thought of as particular. Thinking as such can easily manifest itself into dogmatism. Preemptively one should assume that they bring to the activity certain presuppositions about race, value, and culture, all of which can falsely shape the outcome of the activity. Even the starting point of the thought action must be thoroughly probed to make sure that it is by intent. For example, Locke assumes that, "Man does not, cannot, live in a valueless world."[23] But this notion must be kept in tension with his cultural pluralist and value relativist perspective. So then, given this information, how might Locke think in terms of value and culture? Simple, Locke thought that we cannot assume our own culture to be the pinnacle of all cultures. He also thought that we should be advised that when we do not remember that all cultures are amalgamated events, terribly negative reactions to other cultures can be the result. In essence, these reactions are to other people.

Most importantly, where this book is concerned, Alain Locke's philosophical move, which portends the natural conclusion that racism can be easily understandable as extending from the development of cultural chauvinism. This is a straightforward extrapolation from Locke's arguments on the matter of culture and values. Locke's invitation to consider racism as developing from a misapprehension of the value of Black culture, as well as other cultures, also demonstrates that racism observed through this framework is a type of cultural ignorance. In this sense, the oppressed class can also participate in the ignorance of the oppressor class, through their lack of attention or even outright dismissal of their own culture. Locke was in no way immune from engaging in this type of dismissive behavior. Locke's own comments on the subject of other Black people, particularly when he took them to be uneducated, displayed an explicit class bias, at minimum.[24] This bias is found in his early years, but also continues through to his later years. The question could absolutely and possibly should be put to those who position his historical importance as the unquestionable "Father of the Harlem Renaissance," what damage was incurred by Locke's bias due to his place of prominence during that period?

While it is true that Locke was instrumental in shepherding the Harlem Renaissance, it is equally true that with his voice being the loudest, in terms of what counted for the birth or rebirth of the New Negro, certain other viewpoints remained silenced except only to artists and academics. Understanding value as essentially a problem for thought derived from being linked to culture, exposes certain presuppositions which Locke held, that are exclusive in relation to other ways to view value and shifts in value. If someone held a similar opinion about value as Locke, they could be of the belief that white people were unaware of the significance of the creative talent and production of Black people. And, if this evaluative deficit were remedied, then it would probably cause white people to reassess their position concerning the value of Black people as a cultural grouping, meaning they would come to see Black people as equals. Although Locke, in later speeches given in Haiti in 1943, also considered the socioeconomic modality of the nation, he did seem to recognize white people as being aware of Black people's creative productions. Also, this type of knowledge does not reduce the need that capitalists have for workers who can be exploited. One statement that typifies Locke's thoughts on this matter is, "Only cultural parochialism stands between us and this larger perspective; and when we finally outgrow such subjective limitations, a new panorama of the past and of the future of mankind will open out before our enlightened eyes."[25] During Locke's life, Black people, being especially understood as easily exploitable due to a national racist indoctrination, were certainly considered as an option for exploitable workers. So, this exposure of Locke's presuppositions does not preclude value from being a problem for thought, but it does convey that the knowledge of value along with socioeconomic conditions does not necessarily create a greater possibility for the development of solutions for a flourishing lived experience of Black people.

In 1930 Locke drafted an article, "The Contribution of Race to Culture," in which he asked the poignant question, "can we have the advantages of cultural differences without their obvious historical disadvantages?"[26] This article and the question more specifically gains importance when it is kept in tension with the truth that some variation of this article was published by Locke at least three times. The major point of the argument that Locke puts forth in the article turns on the notion that all cultures are amalgamations of other cultures, therefore no culture should develop a chauvinistic attitude toward other cultures. Locke's suggested solution is to do away with proprietorship and vested interest. In doing so, it was his opinion that an atmosphere of "limitless interchangeability" would develop.[27] It is not obvious in this article, or any other of his articles, that he has intently performed a deep investigative probe into the political economy of the day, to determine if it were even possible to have the type of interchangeability he suggests while maintaining such a system. of course it could be asked how would the article be different if this were the case. If this were the case, the way in which Locke charted the experience of Black people and therefore the substance of Black art would require a different lens. Also, "who or what is Negro," is certainly a different question, even though the grouping would be the same. Again, the evaluative lens would be different. One major difference that might arise from the exposing of things forced upon Black people legally instead of culturally is that might have caused Locke to refrain from using only one focus, the changing of white people's attitudes toward Black people, as the major catalytic component of certain undesirable responses. This focus should not be singular, and must be kept in tension with other foci that provide whatever information available about the experiential world of Black people, if real-world change is the aim.

VALUE AS A PROBLEM OF HUMAN EXISTENCE

Hubert Harrison makes a significant attempt at keeping just this sort of tension applied in his activities, writings and otherwise. This is significant because he was an organic scholar and a contemporary of Alain Locke. An early demonstration of this tension is found in a 1904 letter to the editor of the *New York Times* in response to the long-held stereotype that all Black people stole chickens. It is quite easy to see how such a stereotype as this serves the purpose of devaluing an entire group of people. It does the work of encapsulating Black people with the label of criminal. The stereotype depicts Black people as thieves, and not as having some people that steal within their ranks. If the essence of Black people is to steal or any other criminal behavior, then a credible argument could be made that they should be treated accordingly by the police and possibly local vigilantes like Southern lynch mobs. Such a claim, if it were proven to be true, would indicate that neither education, counseling, religion, or any other attempt to change Black people would end beyond utter futility, because it would be their nature to be criminal. While there are a few subscribers to this obnoxious opinion, even average educated people know that there does not exist an essence of criminal behavior among Black people. First of all, criminality is determined by the state. Beyond this important point, Harrison's critique captured the intent of the article by understanding the value gap[28] he created. The *New York Times* article was not only informing white people to think a certain way about Black people, but it was also any justifying negative actions made toward Black people by white people. Thus, he was perceptive in pointing out that, in this instance, value or the lack of value was a problem of human existence.

Hubert Harrison's perceptivity did not end with a mere response to the New York Times concerning chicken theft. By 1919, he was briefly the editor of the *New Negro* journal. This journal was created as a tool for lifting the consciousness of all people of color, particularly Black people. What is notable about the journal, in consideration of value as a problem of human existence, is Harrison's identification of the New Negro as a group. It is in this journal that, perhaps for the first time ever, we see the nomenclature "New Negro" used in print. What is more interesting, in relation to this current work, is the separation in Harrison's notion of the New Negro and the same notion in the writings of Alain Locke. The distance between the ideas and the things that ground their ideas is quite apparent. For Harrison, the description of the Negro as new was in connection with the willingness of Black people to defend themselves from the terrorism of white people during the Red Summer in 1919.[29] The New Negro was a radical, in the eyes of Harrison, based upon the different outcomes Harrison and others were witnessing in terms of the recent encounters Black people had with whites. The New Negro was suitably "Negro first, Negro last, and Negro always."[30] This New Negro in Harrison's description is not seeking to prove her value or educate white people concerning how to think about her value. They simply wanted equal justice before the law. But the New Negro, according to Alain Locke, was as much about youth as it was fresh ideas attached to urban spaces. Appropriately, for Alain Locke, Black people were becoming more self aware and were beginning to demonstrate the type of agency necessary to meet the challenges of their modernity while intentionally turning their backs on their past enslavement. But for Harrison, it was the very memory of past enslavement and ongoing racist treatment that furnished the impetus of the New Negro to stand firm on the simple claim of never again.

The connection of the social to the economic lens through which Harrison launched his ideas were pervasive throughout his writings. One example of this type of connection is found in a 1926 (September) review of Carl Van Vechten's dubiously titled book, *Nigger Heaven*. Harrison's review was entitled, "Homo Africanus Harlemi," which was a title meant to display contempt for the associates of Van Vechten, by offering a thinly veiled allusion to their performing as minstrels. In November of the same year, Harrison wrote on the same subject, only this time it was in form of a response to those who reviewed his review. The significance here is that in these reviews Harrison puts forth an argument about the validity of Van Vechten's book which hangs on Harrison's notion of truth and his concept of integrity. His notion of truth was in reference to the picture that Van Vechten painted of Black people. While, his concept of integrity was attached to his critique of other reviewers whose intent was to only heap praise onto the book negating any critical perspective.

Truth, in this respect, is encapsulated in this statement by Harrison on the matter, "I rest my critical opinion of its literary merits on its artistic excellence, as form, and on its sociologic truth, or lack of it; and this must be buttressed by my own independent knowledge." Additionally, he continued, "I condemned Van Vechten's book as a poor specimen of literary craftsmanship, and on the further ground that it is a viciously false picture of the life which he pretends to depict."[31] The sociologic factors to which Harrison refers are the basic sociological factors of human life in community, such as family structure, religious beliefs, and the means of production. Truth from this perspective cannot rise above the lived experience of the people as identified by scientific methods with consideration given to the politics of the day. Integrity, for Harrison, extends from his idea of truth. This simply means that the people who lacked integrity were those Black people and others who were supporters of Van Vechten's book in spite of the inherent misrepresentations they knew were present. Truth and integrity as determinants for value particularly as it pertains to the African American struggle and through an ethnic reflective frame is demonstrative of good and bad or helpful and harmful. In this sense, the same sentiment is shared by Du Bois in his "Criteria for Negro Art," where he discloses a belief that all art is propaganda either for or against Black people. Both Du Bois and Harrison knew that the lack of criticism Van Vechten received was due to certain Black people taking a functionalist or pragmatic approach when it came to the production of Black Art. There was the belief from Locke and others that at least one function of the art they produced was to please white donors. This belief, according to Harrison and

Du Bois, was detrimental to value which could clearly be seen by them as a matter of freedom and death, and not merely a matter just for thought.

The distance created between the ideas of Locke to Harrison present a certain type of ideological polarity concerning the function of value in terms of Black people and the freedom struggle. However, there is middle ground. William Henry Ferris, a Harvard and Yale trained philosopher, presents the case for grappling with value from an existential idealist point of view. In volume 1 of his book, *The African Abroad*, he throws light on being a Black scholar at the dawning of the twentieth century. By doing so, he was drawing a connection between his particular life and his idealist understanding of all human life in a universal sense. He weighs his hopes and dreams for himself against what he takes to be a providential nature to the universe. Although, he presents a forward and upward progression to the movement of time, there is a sense by which the reader can gather his disappointment and his struggle to cope with his lived experience as a Black scholar. He wrote, "I had dreamed of teaching colored students in college metaphysics and the philosophy of knowledge, but in this little volume I will teach the Negro race the philosophy of life." If the reader was not able to decipher the intent or aim of his book from certain of the half steps he takes, Ferris spells it out clearly by providing what he thinks of the Black condition and his intent in terms of this as an overt blow toward disrupting the hindrances to a flourishing life for Black people, particularly Black thinkers.

In spite of his espousal of the notion that the experiential shift in society being as upward in nature or toward a flourishing aim for humanity, he never once neglected to spell how this upward nature was at the expense of Black pain, especially the pain of the Black idealist. What separated Ferris from Locke was his intentional effort to write for and to a Black audience. His goal in this sense is not only to expose the meaning of blackness at the dawning of the twentieth century, but to also awaken the sleeping Black masses from their slavery of the mind. Being a member of Marcus Garvey's United Negro Improvement Association (UNIA), he most certainly would have imbibed the notion that Black people had to "emancipate [themselves] from mental slavery, none but [theirselves] can free [their] minds."[32] However, the separation between Ferris and Harrison was based upon the former's appeal to idealism and the latter's use of socialism. This point is at least equally as important, if not more, as Ferris's focus on Black people. Harrison aimed his writings to the Black masses or the οι πολλοι, while Ferris was imbued by Du Bois's notion of the Talented Tenth, and being an idealist, he held that it was the elite or οι αριστοι, as far as their intelligence, that would lead the change of the world for the better through the living out of high ideals. In this sense, Ferris could be rightly classified as an elitist, which might explain why Harrison displayed disdain for his style of writing, as noted in a diary entry.[33]

To fully understand Ferris is to first understand that he subscribed to a type of dialectical idealism, which in the philosophical sense it is meant that he gave credence to the notion that the ongoing phenomenon in the universe is the product of a mind revealing itself. Accordingly, this mind is the mind of an immanent God.[34] However, one should not read Ferris as positing that the end of the story is already written. Ferris makes a distinction which must be kept in tension with his idealist leanings. Voluntarism was a significant component of Ferris's version of dialectical idealism. This concept is summarized in the phrase, "where there is a will there is a way." For Ferris, history could not be understood unless the human being was understood to be an ethical, aesthetical, and religious being.[35] He took history to be a study of the development of the free spirit of humans.[36] Ferris saw the lack of belief, by Black people, in their intrinsic value as humans as causal to the lack of belief in possibility; which is a problem for human flourishing. He knew this also to be a problem for human existence. So he proffered an idealist argument against pessimism, and foreshadowed a critique which can be used today against what is referred to as Afro-pessimism.

For Ferris, there was a necessity to recapture the full historic picture in order to make a correct assessment about future possibilities. George Trumball Ladd, a professor of Ferris's while he was a student at Yale, taught that, "Man's philosophy, his science, his art, his ethics, and religion are not caused by mechanical forces external to himself; but they arise out of the depth of the human soul."[37] This point was not lost on Ferris. Many of the people, particularly Black people, had been taught to make assessments about Black people's possibilities based upon their meager existence while in slavery, but for Ferris, this was an incomplete picture. Therefore, in spite of Ferris's reliance on a type of Hegelian method, he must be understood to be a type of undoing of Hegel's historical portrait of the way things were and the way history was unfolding. For Hegel, Africa was the dark continent and without notable contribution to humanity. This was evil to Ferris.[38] For Ferris, an unfolding of the historical narrative of the type Hegel described could only be fully captured conceptually when accounting for the spiritual strivings of the iteration of humanity found in the Black people of America. To know human history in this sense was to know the history of Black people while also mapping their trajectory. Given these parameters, the human story sometimes has pain and deep contrition but also has uplift and victory. This sentiment is expressed even in the view Ferris had of his own life shared in this statement, "I had dreamed of teaching colored students in college metaphysics and the philosophy of knowledge, but in this little volume I will teach the Negro race the philosophy of life."[39]

The philosophy of life he intended to teach was woven together in a tapestry of names from history for which race played little or no role at all in their contribution to humanity. They simply were above race.[40] Ferris believed in the importance of sharing this philosophy of life and motivating others to take up the same quest because he believed this quest to be consistent with being human. Ferris felt that this philosophy of life or what he took to be philosophy in earnest demonstrated or made visible those things which are truly important and have value for life, or make life worth living. Therefore, for Ferris the problem of value or nonbelief in one's own value was truly a problem for human existence. It was evil and disconnected humans from humanity. In other words, it disconnected humans from human possibility based upon human will and life's trajectory. Of value, Ferris quoted James Hutchinson Sterling, "what is peculiarly human is not live in towns with soldiers and police, etc., safely to masticate his victuals; what is peculiarly human is to perceive the apparition of the Universe; what is peculiarly human is to interrogate this apparition, is to ask in its regard, what?—whence?—why?—whither?"[41]

FREEDOM GAZING

When considering this triad of "New Negro" thinkers,[42] in spite of the divergent paths of their philosophical writings, the shape and form of their freedom gazing can be said to have focused their thoughts on the awakening of the consciousnesses within the masses of Black people, either directly or indirectly.[43] Not limiting their actions to this particular effort but simply putting forward that this was an area to which they placed an inordinate amount of stress. This was such a focus or derivative feature that this type of focus has been given a name, contributionism or racial vindicationism.[44] Contributionism in reference to the African American freedom struggle is thought to be the beating back or disrupting of the concept that Black people, Negroes or Africans, never contributed anything to modern civilization. This stress was carried out by researching these contributions and also writing about them. They also lectured about the significance of these historical contributions. This is the thinking from which the holiday we refer to as Black History Month arose.[45] The goal was to develop a perceptual framework within Black people, a way of viewing themselves, that was strong enough to resist the view of Black people's inferiority, which implied they were otherwise disposable and only existed as a means, not as an end.

I think it fair to point out at this juncture that none of the three members of this ad hoc triad I have constructed for the purpose of analysis saw the cultivating of intellect within the Black masses as reducible to a function of only educational institutions. In fact, I think it is also safe to say that the function in which they saw themselves to be engaged was not one that they took to have any resolution. In other words, they felt as if this effort would always be necessary as a constitutive part of what makes individuals and communities free. This belief was already inherently replete with the understanding that to exist as human meant coming to a true knowledge of the self and community in time and space. This to say that for this type of knowledge to be present, a correct picture of history is required as well as an accounting for present conditions which both enhance and limit one's ability to flourish. In this sense, knowledge was not just for knowledge's sake. Knowledge, as they saw it, was for the explicit purpose of living, living well, and living better.[46]

An example of this effort found in the writings of Harrison is his chapter "Education and the Race." Harrison wrote, "With most of the present sources of power controlled by the white race it behooves my race as well as the other subject races to learn the wisdom of the weak and to develop to the fullest that organ whereby weakness has been able to overcome strength; namely the intellect."[47] It is clear from this that Harrison considered the cultivation of the intellect or intellection as the requisite wisdom to overcome oppression. However, Harrison should not be read in isolation as an aberration within his milieu. He was a member of a tradition in which the lifting or raising of consciousness was not just morally correct, it was taken to be an unavoidable responsibility. Therefore, in spite of the prominent statute Harrison and the others maintained, they were not unique. There were literary clubs, college sororities and fraternities, debate societies, history clubs, and many other similarly focused groups.[48]

What is significant about these three thought leaders as it pertains to this text, in light of their focus upon intellection as a tool against oppression, is the connection that can be made to DuBois's notion of the scholar activist mentioned earlier in this text. Their encouragement to read was not simply for the purpose of gaining better employability; it was aimed at better participation in the reshaping or transforming of society. This transformation was to provide a place for them to live and thus to be free. Transformation of society might, today, seem too lofty a goal for such a minority, recently released from slavery and currently under such a oppressive regime, but these men were committed to becoming the "old Negro." Upward and onward was the only direction to travel. What this meant was that their struggle for freedom was obligatory. Just as Du Bois and Crummell before them had given their lives to the uplift of Black people, the freedom gaze as a perceptual framework compelled them to do the same. To this point Ferris would say, "Upon this volume, I will stake my youthful dreams and experiences."[49] They could see no other goal, and even if freedom was only a presupposition, it would be through the lens of this presupposition that they would translate the meaning of humanity.

ETHNIC REFLECTIVE CANON

Ferris's presentation of this philosophy of life within the context of his particular narrative, the inclusion of Black people within it, and the manner of this inclusion, was monumental for the year 1913. The use of his title alone, "The African Abroad," during this period reframes and reshapes the mode of perception in which Black people, whether in the United States or elsewhere, were to be viewed beyond the continent of Africa. Clearly, Ferris's two volume book, along with the works of Locke and Harris, were within the bounds of the Ethnic Reflective canon. In this capacity, Ferris and the others certainly provided an expansion for the conception of blackness while at the same time highlighting their lived experience. Their example, together with those that came before, did not go unnoticed. Others throughout the African diaspora began to take note. Of specific importance is the Negritude movement, which was begun in France by French-speaking students from French Africa, the French West Indies (Martinique, Guadeloupe, and Haiti), and French Guiana in South America. The major figures were Aimé Césaire, Leopold Sedar Senghor, and Leon Damas, who, among others, found community in their communal heritage and the feeling of cultural isolation.[50] These students realized that the very French culture that they were studying was responsible for the tragic and impoverished existence of the people in their homelands.

Negritude was at once an expression of the richness of blackness and an expression of the otherness created by white colonizers and oppressors. The alterity these whites constructed was resisted physically by those in the homelands of members within the negritude movement. But these young Black students at the Sorbonne, following the lead of such poets as Claude McKay, Countee Cullen, Langston Hughes, Jean Toomer, Sterling Brown, and others were beginning to give verbal signification to what could be called the souls of Black folk. In many ways the Negritude movement was the root of modern existentialism, being a response to the alienated position of Blacks in history.[51] What is noticeable in viewing negritude thinkers parallel to the thinkers from the New Negro Movement is the undeniable interconnected nature of the two fronts of movement. The oneness of the movement is not found in a singularity of ideas, but instead it is seen in the development of a humanistic philosophy focused on the things that thwart a flourishing human existence. Their desires for freedom, their belief in the innate value of Black humanity and their faith in the possibility of a flourishing lived experience were all consistent existential concerns subsumed into a developing philosophy of the Black experience. Although different approaches were used to address these concerns, from pragmatic accommodationist thinkers who wanted peace at all costs to radical socialist thinkers who took rebellion or revolution to be viable approaches, these existential concerns remained prominent.

With the prominence of these existential concerns came the recurrence of certain ideological trends or philosophical thought patterns. Idealism, socialism, and pragmatism were among the most prominent of these philosophical thought patterns. In the past, certain of these trends were labeled according to their primary concerns, such as accommodationist, integrationist, nationalist, and Ethiopic or emigrationist. However, in consideration of the ethnic reflective canon in relation to these trends, while also thinking of them as philosophical trends, it is the second-order concerns that have provided the prompting through which they were labeled. In the past, researchers have typically focused on the immediate problem that was being addressed by the individual and never gave any consideration to their mode of reflective thought. The former categorizations were indicative of this shortsighted approach which reduced the individual thinkers to people of their time while at the same time implicitly describing them as irrelevant to any other period. This partially explains their disappearance from present-day academic studies. Of course, anti-Black racism has to account for much of this responsibility. But, the point still remains that if Du Bois is basically an integrationist, then he does not have to be mentioned when discussing other socialists. In fact, only recently have the socialists taken very limited notice of Hubert Harrison. Booker T. Washington is only thought to be an accommodationist, receiving no attention from pragmatists. And certainly, William Ferris does not get any nods from the idealists. These thinkers did attempt address their immediate concerns; however, they also made a considerable effort to think about the best manner in which to think about these concerns.

By focusing on the second-order reflections of these thinkers, a better assessment can be made of their work, while at the same time determinations can be made about their usefulness for similar trends found today. Why is it important that their absence be exposed? In similar manner and for similar reasons, the same sort of thing happens to philosophically minded Black thinkers of today. They are either not read or read as if the answers they provide are only particular rather than universalizeable. Also, Black thinkers themselves simply regurgitate contemporary philosophical claims as if no one has attempted to respond to a similar problem in the past. In consideration of the previously mentioned philosophical trends, it is interesting to note that in the triad mentioned in this chapter, each took the problem of value, but Locke was a pragmatist, Ferris was an idealist, and Harrison was a materialist. The significance of their divergent methods is found in the later thinkers who took up the same problems. While the major Negritude thinkers, Senghor, Césaire, and Damas, took their cues from Du Bois and Locke, they were each idealist thinkers. Claudia Jones, a newspaperwoman similar to Ida B. Wells-Barnett, did not follow Wells-Barnett's pragmatic leanings, but instead became a student of Du Bois and leaned left, way left. In fact she is buried to the left of Karl Marx as a demonstration of her radical ideology. The point here is that in the modern era, although the existential concerns may have been the same, the disposition of the thinker was not determined or reducible to their skin or their influences. They were human and just as any other group of philosophically minded thinkers are understood to possess a certain level of complexity. The same is true of Black thinkers during the modern era of the African American freedom struggle.

MOVEMENT MAP

Table 3.1: A Chart of the Ideas of the Freedom Movement——> Ferris, Harrison, and Locke

	CD/ST	Humanistic Expression
Freedom		
Revolution	H	H, F
Rebellion	F	L
Peace	L	

NOTES

1. Community Development/Social Transformation activities = struggling for freedom

2. William Julius Moses, *Creative Conflict African American Thought* (Cambridge: Cambridge, 2004), pp. 121–138.

3. Robert H. Brisbane, *The Black Vanguard: Origins of the Negro Social Revolution, 1900–1960* (Valley Forge, PA: Judson, 1970), p. 18.

4. Hoffer, *Plessy v. Ferguson*, 41.

5. Jonathan Holloway, *Confronting the Veil* (Chapel Hill: University of North Carolina Press, 2002), p. 22.

6. Kevin Gaines, *Uplifting the Race* (Chapel Hill: University of North Carolina Press, 1996), p. 101; Holloway, *Confronting the Veil*, p. 19.

7. Holloway, *Confronting the Veil*, p. 19.

8. Tommy J. Curry, *The Philosophical Treatise of William H. Ferris* (London: Rowman & Littlefield, 2016), p. 6.

9. Ferguson and McClendon, *African American Philosophers and Philosophy* (London: Bloomsbury, 2019), p. 196.

10. Gaines, *Uplifting the Race*, p. 42.

11. Holloway, *Confronting the Veil*, p. 22.

12. Ferguson and McClendon, *African American Philosophers and Philosophy*, p. 40.
13. Kevin Gaines, *Uplifting the Race*, p. 42.
14. Ibid.
15. In the presence of other intellectuals ...
16. Their question was the question of the Negro as a problem or what is the meaning of Blackness? (phenomenological-how does it feel to be a problem?)
17. L. Harris, "Alain Locke and Community."
18. Ibid.
19. J. C. Stewart, and A . L. Locke, eds., *Race Contacts and Interracial Relations* (Washington, DC: Howard University Press, 1992).
20. L. E. Wright, "Alain Locke and Race."
21. Race as a social construct ...
22. Harris, *Locke*, p. 201.
23. Harris, *Locke*, p. 34.
24. Locke's letter to his mom ...
25. Jacoby Adeshei Carter, *African American Contributions to the Americas' Cultures: A Critical Edition of Lectures by Alain Locke* (New York: Palgrave, 2016), p. 11.
26. Harris, *Locke*, p. 203.
27. Ibid.
28. Glaude, *Begin Again*, pp. 23–24.
29. Rayford Logan, *The Betrayal of the Negro: From Rutherford Hayes to Woodrow Wilson* (London: Collier, 1969), pp. 341–354.
30. *A Hubert Harrison Reader*, p. 98.
31. Ibid., p. 345.
32. Marcus Garvey, author, Robert A. Hill and Barbara Bair (eds.), *The Marcus Garvey and Universal Negro Improvement Association Papers*, Vol. VII: November 1927–August 1940; p. 791.
33. *A Hubert Harrison Reader*, p. 185.
34. For a more detailed discussion on the influences upon Ferris's thinking, the reader should refer to Tommy J. Curry's edited work on William Ferris. Tommy J. Curry, ed., *The Philosophical Treatise of William H. Ferris: Selected Readings from the African Abroad or, His Evolution in Western Civilization*, 2016.
35. Ferris, *African Abroad*, p. 26.
36. Ibid.
37. Ibid., p. 27.
38. Ibid., p. 132.
39. Ibid., p. 132.
40. Ibid., p. 139.
41. Ibid., p. 179.
42. This is not to suggest by any means that they were the only ones of this sort.
43. Locke leaned more indirectly ...
44. Ferguson, *Philosophy of African American Studies*, p. 98.

45. Carter G. Woodson organized the Association for the Study of Negro Life in 1915. Ibid., p. 161.

46. Whitehead, *The Function of Reason*, p. 8.

47. *When Africa Awakes*, p. 123.

48. Wilson J. Moses, "The Lost World of the Negro, 1895–1919: Black Literary and Intellectual before Renaissance," *African American Review*.

49. Ferris, *African Abroad*, p. 132.

50. Edward Allen Jones, *Voices of Negritude*, p. 14.

51. https://www.blackpast.org/global-african-history/negritude-movement/.

Chapter 4

From Montgomery to West Africa

"You—you are not niggers. You—you are not slaves. You are God's children."[1] This powerful statement is used by Howard Thurman repeatedly throughout his many writings. His multiple uses of the statement is an act which I explain as an attempt to put forth his notion of how Black people should comport themselves in the face of any dehumanizing oppression. Another way to understand what is meant is as follows: greater is that which is within me then that which appears to the world, or blackness does not explain me. To place it in the vernacular, one might say, I am a bigger figure than being a nigger. Black skin has no essential nature. However, due to social constriction, there is an underlying essence to the experience of blackness. This is the intent of the epigraphs above. Although Negritude thinkers made attempts to capture the essence of blackness within their poetic writings, while also referencing the prior works by Black writers in America, the literary movement in Harlem was not essentialist in nature in any unified way. Some of its proponents could be characterized in this manner, but the movement as a whole was in many ways a continuation of the American Negro Academy, which was anything but unified on the matter. It was Du Bois in particular who intimated that whites created the conditions for certain behaviors to appear and then criticized Black people, especially poor Black people, for displaying the very same behaviors. This was his assessment in the Philadelphia Negro. While demonstrating the thread of continuity that extended from Du Bois and others through the Civil Rights moment of the Freedom Movement, in this chapter the question of "what has my blackness (otherness, alterity, separateness) done to me?," and through inference "what does oppression do to a society?" will form the background of this portion of the discussion. The triad of Nkrumah, Thurman, and King will be used in this chapter to gain the ability to define a path of entrance into an understanding of how these particular questions were thought about during their moment. In using the triad in this manner, the aim of this discussion will be to indicate the reality of an effect of oppression on Black people and on society at large without presupposing the ability to determine in this space an exact quantitative measure of the effect. Despite this usage of the triad as a focal point for covering ground toward the aim, others of their contemporaries, just as in previous chapters, in the continued effort to reveal the notion that these thinkers were participating in an extended struggle for freedom, known here as the freedom movement, through their intentional freedom gazing.

These questions taken together form the boundary upon which the problem of the color line rests. Within these questions, there are formative issues which must be considered if these questions are to be responded to completely. Among these formative issues are economic, educational, and health issues. I am using formative here in the sense of a development which has lasting implications such that Black Studies, Africana Studies, or African American Studies cannot be fully attended to without first offering consideration to what problems they address in terms of value, while also giving thought to what would count as an adequate response in terms of epistemology, and lastly it must be considered how this response might be gained in terms of method.[2] In other words, these questions and their general target of oppression, but more specifically racial oppression, assist in determining the quality and credence of all humanistic studies, either through their neglect or through serious attention. Especially in an admittedly existential account such as this text, it is necessary to acknowledge the "why" of my framing in terms the consideration I give to the ethnic reflective canon, the freedom gaze, and blackness as a human problem. However, due to the perennial nature of oppression, any description offered must always be revisited.

It cannot be overstated that while there exists within this text a certain historical progression, it is not the intent of the author that the book be considered as necessarily a history book. The intent is to engage in a philosophical discussion about how a certain historical moment within the freedom struggle of people of African descent in the Americas might be considered. To this point, philosophy in general is defined by certain big questions or questioning techniques, with specific genres of philosophy being defined by certain fundamental questions. So then, what could count as one of the fundamental questions for an African American philosophy? Again, one such question that might arise, when the genre is viewed from the perspective of certain existential concerns, is how has living in an oppressive environment affected me? (Has it affected my will to be and my becoming? Does it play a role in human fragmentation?) This question is also fundamental to the concerns of this chapter along with the development of this question in African American thought. Ideas contained within African American thought will be examined for certain cleavages in meaning. Also, certain experiential moments will be examined for significance. Additionally, there will be a considerable amount of attention placed upon the shift from a view of cultural aesthetics within the existential crisis of blackness to a focus upon the existential crisis of fragmentation of the individual and the community.

War, the Great Depression, and war once more were catalysts to major shifts in the deep structure of the Black community. These types of experiential moments, particular to the era of investigation, must be kept in tension with considerations about the nature of racism in this type of discussion. African American philosophy is trending toward neglect in this area. This neglect can be thought to have correspondence in a direct sense to the relationship between the philosophers who give consideration to these types of discussions and the general trend in philosophic education today. In this current moment, there is little focus within philosophic eduction placed upon the issues to which Black thinkers and specifically Black philosophers have in the past brought to the fore. These would be the issues which thwart Black existence. A possible factor in this occurrence may have something to do with the blind spots created by specificity of training. Specificity of training creates a narrowness of focus beneficial for scholarly production but not necessarily beneficial for grappling with perennial questions of human existence. Another possible factor has much to do again with the problem of blind spots, but not the blind spots created by academic training.[3] The blind spots to which I am currently referring are associated with class consciousness and fragmentation. Many philosophers, particularly Black philosophers, along with other Black scholars, are no longer concerned with the problems of the Black masses, and are instead concerned with the problems with which the majority within the discipline are concerned. That is to say, instead of answering the problems of blackness as an existential crisis, they concern themselves with the problems of philosophy. About the matter, Lewis Gordon says,

> There was a time, that is, when these areas of philosophy produced groundbreaking ideas, but their adherents now produce professionals who collapse into an endless stream of repeatable practices guided by the same forces as entertainment at one extreme and radical non-emergence at the other.[4]

The experiential moment that will provide grounding for the launching of this section is World War II. Details about the war and the involvement of Black soldiers are plentiful and I will not attempt here to inadequately depose the historical record of this event. However, focus upon the effect of this event on the oppressed is necessary, particularly upon the effect on African Americans, such that the triad chosen and their discussion on alterity can be understood within the proper frame. Just as mentioned previously in chapter two, to study consciousness, it is necessary to study the effect; therefore, shifts in consciousness require similar attention. After World War II, there was an apparent shift in consciousness within the African diaspora identifiable in the production of anticolonial literature.[5] Another factor in the creation of the shift in consciousness has to do with variance of within the community of Black people. For example, many who participated in the war were able to receive veterans benefits. Others moved to the North to take manufacturing jobs which had been vacated by whites during the war. Accordingly, education, housing, healthcare, and employment were all affected. A growing divide was widening even within the Black community. Of the writings in anticolonial literature, many are significant and continue to have lasting impact, but in order to preface the focus upon this chapter's triad, I center the discussion around two books with other writings offering peripheral structure. The use of these particular books is premised on the description they put forward of the attitude of the diaspora in this period.

In 1948, Oliver Cromwell Cox, a Trinidadian-American scholar and professor of sociology, wrote a detailed study, *Caste, Class, and Race*. Cox carefully outlined the attributes of his three topics of study and distinguished one from the other while also settling upon a stable and standard definition for each. At the core, the text is Marxian analysis of these three topics while focusing on the social condition found within United States in his chosen period. He also extrapolated the data to make bold predictions for the future of the American social structure. Cox's Trinidadian heritage could be deemed by some as a stumbling block as it pertains to understanding his inclusion in the ethnic reflective canon of the modern era of the African American freedom struggle, but I should clarify why his inclusion makes sense. The first point is that there does become a moment when African American culture is influenced in vast ways from members across the African diaspora. However, during the period that Cox wrote the text, the influence upon the experience of being Black in America from across the diaspora was minimal, at most. Secondly, upon reading the book, one quickly notices that the group under analysis is Black people in the United States. It is not my purpose to play down the Caribbean and African influence on the freedom struggle in America, but what is of note is that Cox makes a salient point that must be considered when interrogating whether it is possible and when it is necessary to collapse the freedom struggles throughout the diaspora into one analytic study. Cox informs the reader that American Black people did not exists as a colony or a caste and therefore they were not a homogenous grouping similar to other peoples who experienced oppression across the diaspora. Unlike many other spaces which were inhabited by the diaspora and even those colonized spaces on the continent of Africa, Black people in America simply could not be decolonized, especially in the same fashion that was beginning to occur around the time of Cox's writing and following. The existential conditions were simply not the same. A better analogy through which to understand these freedom movements across the diaspora is a cascading effect in a phenomenon like waves. A similar phenomenon transpires during the moment known as the Renaissance. The Florentine Renaissance begins before the German Renaissance and for different reasons with differing consequences. They can also be spoken of separately.

The beginning of Cox's book locates the moment of analysis as the period immediately following World War II. The importance of knowing this location is that Cox makes it clear that it is consistent with his finding that the war was a major catalytic factor in the conditions that were driving that specific moment within his frame of analysis. In the attempt to understand the previously mentioned boundary setting questions, "what has my blackness (otherness, alterity, separateness) done to me?," and through inference "what does oppression do to a society?," It is this type of study that is essential, especially for fields such as philosophy to maintain contact with material reality through a deep structured analysis of social structures along with political economy. Also, the conclusions attained provide the boundary necessary to frame my assessment of the period. From Cox, we receive a perspective that is social in nature. His concern, which has everything to do with the focus of this chapter, is to demonstrate what oppression understood as antagonism does to a society. The imagery he enlists in the beginning to carry his meaning is the imagery of war. In using this imagery, Cox distinguishes between the wars that occurred before capitalism and those that occurred afterward. It suffices to say, after capitalism, there exist new antagonisms never before present. They came in the form known as political-class wars. One such antagonism, racial antagonism, came into being in the year 1492. It was developed and shaped by the capitalist system. Built into this concept of antagonism is the notion of the political sense of alterity.

Antagonisms as political-class wars have negatively affected the entire society, but the focus of this text extends outwardly from one variety of antagonism upon one group of people and then, from there, the observance of the effect in broad terms will be engaged. In terms of the characteristic or detail of the variety of antagonism to be examined, which is racial antagonism, the substance of alterity understood as otherness or separateness will be placed into perspective by first describing racial antagonism. In describing racial antagonism, the development and necessity of alterity as a weapon for racial antagonists will also be exposed. Racial antagonism is akin to racial hatred.[6] Racial antagonism may stem from ignorance but should not be equated with ignorance, which when seen as ignorance, can seem to be an unintended consequence. Hatred is not unintended, and the actions which arise from hatred are not unintended. However, racial antagonism is also connected to limited access to resources, which is not exactly the same as limited resources.[7] Therefore, the root of racism is always connected to power. Brute power or political class competition determines who can have access and who cannot.

Whenever this type of brute power is used to limit access to resources, it is always a product of the machinations of the political system at work in the particular state. As such, this use of brute power can never be ameliorated without changing the political system of the state. Our political system allows for the use of racial antagonisms to limit access to resources through the politics as usual.

Cox describes racial exploitation and race prejudice as having "developed among Europeans with the rise of capitalism and nationalism," and that "racial antagonism can be traced to the policies and attitudes of leading capitalist people, the white people of Europe and North America."[8] Alterity is inherent to race antagonism, which again is equal to political-class war. In the present system, in order to attain sufficient resources assimilation is required on some level. Great gains require assimilation on higher level. "The most powerful techniques utilized by the white ruling class for the retardation of the races is segregation."[9]

In chapter 2, Du Bois's personal experiential moments are taken up as an existential crisis of humanity which disrupted his thinking regarding the relationship between truth and value. In order to frame the discussion of this matter, it was necessary to expose, in some detail, experiential moments and the variance between Black and blackness. The focus in chapter 2 had at its core the individual, of which the exemplar was Du Bois, but the current discussion in this chapter will be group oriented. Du Bois's question concerning the experience of blackness began in isolation and abstraction, which was the driving factor motivating him to begin with the phrase, "Between me and the other world." For the triad of Thurman, King, and Nkrumah, the exploration of blackness began in community with Black people as an audience. Therefore their crisis was shared by their audience. There is no mention of any bifurcation or duality in their language. For the early Du Bois, there were only two worlds. His world or the Black world and the other world, understood as the white world. The white world was equal to the American world or the world of normative occurrences. However, in the Black world, existence was fragile and death was common. Accordingly, the duality he presented only left two ways of being, and in the early work of Du Bois, it was forced upon the Black person to make an attempt at embodying both ways of being, in spite of their presupposed opposition.

What is commensurably expressed in the late work of Du Bois and in the writings of the current triad is a sense of the loss or limited being or liminal humanity. This is apparent in the title, *The Dusk of Dawn*. In order to gain a better perspective upon the idea presented in the term liminal humanity,[10] Martin Luther King Jr.'s question, "what is man?," from his book *The Measure of Man* will be put forward here, but rephrased as "what have we humans become in the present moment?" In doing so, the concept of time becomes a definite variable that cannot be easily canceled as the solution to this verbal equation is estimated. Even as we move from the universal human to the particular Black person, by asking what does it mean to be Black, there is a unique confrontation with time of which an account must be given. In this sense, the question must always be understood as an attempt to grapple with the meaning of being black at a given moment in a particular place. To this point, I would suggest that there can exist a universal conception of blackness, but it is difficult and perhaps impossible to embody universal blackness. Calypso is simply not the blues, and reggae is not jazz. There are always temporal spatial nuances. Some may argue that hip-hop has managed to do just this, but is hip-hop a Black music form? This is maybe a question for another book, but suffice to say for this work, specificity of blackness is contingent upon a time and space relationship. Time, which denotes change, throws light on possibility which is present in each moment in spite of what is found to be objectionable. However, there is also present the insight found within the moment, which was made clear in the modern era that the experience of blackness was not the fulfillment of potential.

The second book which will be used as the centering ground from which to launch the discussion, in this chapter, is *Black Skin, White Masks* by Frantz Fanon, written in 1952. Separation in the two books is created by, among other things, the distance the authors possess in terms of methods, questions, and commitments. As sociologist or more explicitly a social philosopher, Cox was using methods which provided adequacy and accuracy when exposing certain social phenomenon and the supporting data. He was concerned about questions which could only be disposed of by assessing a large group over a period of time. Cox was too committed to the discovery of those things that created a common understanding around notions of castes, class and race. As a psychiatrist or existentialist thinker committed to using psychoanalytic tools, the scope of Fanon was far narrower than that of Cox. Fanon was concerned with how the effects of blackness on the individual affected the community. He was committed to exposing the damage done while also demonstrating the created nature of the problem, and therefore the damage. Fanon's major aim was to demonstrate how the myth of blackness and of whiteness have disrupted the existence of humanity, but not totally, he hoped.

The consequence of Fanon's argument in this text, is the development of a consciousness of the inescapability that racism and oppression shapes and reshapes the way in which we think about the world. This change or set of changes caused by racism and oppression are accepted involuntarily. And if because of racism and oppression, we see the world through the lens of racism and oppression, we also experience the world through the same framework. This is because of how experiential moments occur as explained in a previous chapter. Accordingly, for Fanon, the world shaped by racism and oppression is inherently bad or less than is possible without, because it is a world where human possibility cannot be fulfilled. We do not exist exterior to our thoughts and experiences in the world, which is where racism and oppression exists. In this way, we are limited by our thoughts and experiences. Fanon demonstrates the depths to which these thoughts and experiences deteriorate a society and causes even new creations to be deformed.

Fanon's chapter "The Fact of Blackness" explains the deformed nature of society through the impact made upon the Black person in the form of an existential crisis. The existential crisis presents itself in the form of a restrictive metaphysics in which the Black person has subjectivity, but the ontology of the white person refuses to give recognition. Recognition in this sense would mean equitability. This type of equitability is impossible in a white-framed metaphysics because the white person owns the metaphysics. As colonizer, oppressor, and conqueror, it is necessary to go beyond merely conquering the land, but the conception of the time and of the space within which the land is located must also be conquered. Otherwise, the conquered and colonized objects would not exist. Therefore, in the white reality subjectivity belongs to white people. Fanon describes this phenomenon as such, "For not only must the Black [person] be Black; [they] must be Black in relationship to the white [person]." In this sense, the very thoughts of Black people must be congruent with the role or space created for them in white society or the whole project falls apart. The Black people of the modern era, especially those who had been to war and then come back into their deformed existence, were refusing to play their created role. This sentiment was spreading among Black people but white people had not yet come to the realization that their created metaphysical construction and ontological classification was losing viability. In this chapter, Fanon repeatedly uses the phrase, "Look, a Negro!" Using repetition in this manner demonstrated the inescapability of the oppressors gaze, which was in opposition to his own freedom gaze. This repetition serves an additional purpose for the Black reader. Its use also demonstrated the inherent necessity of the confrontation in which Black people had to engage because of this inescapability. Any attempt to avoid this confrontation only served to demonstrate an acceptance of the deformed ordering of the white man's society. The deformed ordering confines the Black person into an always already alterity of Blackness.

ALTERITY AND BLACKNESS

Previously, in the last chapter, the reflection upon the negritude writers, who are considered to be a part of the broader ethnic reflective canon in the modern era, displayed their active participation in creating a cultural aesthetic movement in reaction to the alienation felt by Black students from various parts of the Caribbean and Africa, living and studying in French society in the late twenties and thirties. Despite the rejection of any conviction of an essential quality deposited in having black skin as demonstrated above, the notion of cultural isolation they put forward is one I find to be significant when attempting to provide a description of the experience of blackness, particularly in the experiential moment after major wars along with international economic devastation. Otherness or alterity in combination with separateness created an experience for Black people, an experience of blackness, which was inferior to their desired experience or what was thought to be possible. The creative writings of previous decades, produced by Black authors spoke to the imaginings of Black people in this regard, but Black people were not allowed to realize their desires in any real sense.

Black writers in the United States were also beginning to take a special interest in expressing something of what the experience of being a Black person living under tremendously oppressive conditions felt like and could engender in the soul. One writer in particular, Richard Wright, took exception to the notion that it was somehow a duty of the well-adjusted Black person to rid themselves of any ill-feeling they might have toward white people specifically or the nation in general concerning the lack of opportunity they received coupled with the brutality in which they were exposed. Alterity in the form of blackness shifted the experience of being human, while carrying with it a confrontation with a juxtaposed nature of being Black, one that would assist in making white people feel superior. In this sense, whiteness was being created from the identical false notions through which created blackness, only the violent means were missing. Simply put, humanness was being distorted for Black people and white people. Of this, Howard Thurman wrote, "the burden of being Black and the burden of being white is so heavy that it is rare in our society to experience oneself as a human being."[11] Richard Wright managed to capture in words this burden felt by Black people, which thwarted their very ability to fully exist as what they were. They were always drenched by someone else's notion of their humanity merely because of the particular way in which the sun reflected on their skin.

From Richard Wright's confrontation with blackness and his exposition of blackness during his moment in the modern era, it was easy to see his coherence with a tradition, especially in terms of his treatment of his subject matter and in his manner of confrontation. The concern in making this point is not to demonstrate his agreement with any proponent from an earlier moment in the tradition, but to demonstrate that he was responding to the earlier proponents of the tradition. This tradition, of course is the freedom struggle. In his 1901 autobiography, Booker T. Washington repeatedly made the proclamation that he had cleansed himself of all bitterness aimed at white people for the treatment he received while conscripted to the institution of slavery. Seemingly, Washington's purpose in putting forward this claim was maybe to demonstrate that his notion of freedom carried with it the need to absolve anyone who participated in his condition or even further that there was no one or no system at fault. Slavery was just a part of the human condition. Viewed in this manner, he seemed to say that in its aftermath, he nor his oppressor had been affected.

Wright, being aware of this text, certainly could not bring himself to agree with the sentiment. His writing was first and foremost a demonstration of how oppression in the form of alterity reduced the space for the development of humanity in the oppressed. Although, the oppressed could develop their humanity but the corridor for its demonstration is narrow with little light. But, Wright was also saying something to the oppressor. First, he was confronting the oppressor with the realization that the condition of the oppressed was a created condition. Secondly, it was clear that this created or artificial condition begged the question, what kind of people would create and allow such a condition to continue, especially once the effects were known, and in spite of the oppressed having repeatedly demonstrated their humanity even in their narrow corridors. In the first chapter of *Native Son,* in a conversation between the main protagonist, Bigger and his friend Gus, Bigger shares his reflection on the matter of blackness as alterity as such,

> Naw. But I just can't get used to it. . . . I swear to God I can't. I know I oughtn't not think about it, but I can't help it. Every time I think about it I feel like somebody's poking a red-hot iron down my throat. Goddammit, look! We live here and they are live there. We Black and they white. They got things and we ain't. They do things and we can't. It's like living in jail. Half the time I feel like I'm on the outside the world peeping in through a knothole in the fence.[12]

In reading this exchange between Bigger and Gus, it is plain to see that whatever emotions of which Washington worked to rid himself, Wright had worked just as hard to fully display his emotions through his writings. Through Bigger, Wright demonstrated the existence and the nature of reflective introspection from a member of the oppressed. He showed this thought pattern to be all too human, in terms of Bigger's awareness of himself in his condition, and Wright demonstrated through Gus's resignation in responding to Bigger, by saying just don't think about it. This resignation revealed just how much the humanity of the oppressed was being restricted.

In much the same way as Richard Wright; Howard Thurman, Martin Luther King Jr., and Kwame Nkrumah came to the realization of the existence of a blackness undergirded by an oppressive ideology focused on creating a group or class which could be easily exploited. Just as with others, the question immediately rises about Nkrumah and his place in this network of thinkers. Through his own admission, it should be understood that Nkrumah was in the United States to be educated outside the reach of colonial auspices, that is to say, he wanted to be influenced by the education he received. He does; however, say that he taught in the United States also, but the impact on the common Black person and therefore the African American freedom struggle at large during the time of his matriculation seems minimum. Nevertheless, to be fair the impact from others in the diaspora on Black people in the United States is certainly growing during this period and by the sixties, the impact is significant even on the common Black person. Polemics designed to distinguish or dismantle notions of the unity of the movement toward freedom by Black people around the world seem pointless and lack fecundity if the only goal is to stage a space to create a new being upon the earth, the non-African American or the Africana American. But, if the point is to make known something about how we might think about the freedom movement in its American moment, then it seems irrational and historically inaccurate to put forward the notion that African Americans never at any moment developed a distinctive character despite moments of active participation from Black people abroad. If the latter can be said to at least be partly correct, which seems more plausible, then there is no reasonable argument that can be offered to deny the nomenclature the "modern era of the African American freedom struggle," while continuing to recognize the emergent benefit of other actors.

The motivation for bringing clarity to this issue has to do specifically with the book by Nkrumah, *Consciencism*, in which he wrestles with the nature and effect of colonialism on the African. Of course, by African he means the continental African or Black person, but the importance of this text in this writing is its timing coupled with the subject matter. Nkrumah's educational experience in America, both in the classroom and out, were instrumental in providing him with the tools to bring pressure on the colonial structure in his own nation. It's an easy leap of logic to find similarities between Jim Crow in the South and the British Colonials in Ghana. As such, the realization that education would be fundamental to the Ghanaian struggle in a similar manner as it was fundamental in this modern moment in the African American struggle was quite apparent. Of course, this education would have to be relevant in terms of information disseminated and problems or questions addressed. Nkrumah seized on this issue, making considerable use of his training in philosophy, he pointed out that without due attention to one's own circumstances, the oppressed student simply becomes a sycophant for the same ideas applied in the same manner as the oppressor. Doing so, merely means that the oppression or colonial domination[13] is allowed to continue, unbothered by the threat of dissent. In this sense, the effect of Blackness[14] or oppression on the nonthinking, nonsuspecting African, or Black person in a broader sense, is they become a vessel for the oppressor's ideological weaponry.

"The dynamics of power shape public education."[15] It was for a reason such as this that Kwame Nkrumah left the Gold Coast[16] for the United States in 1935, residing in Philadelphia until 1945. After that period, he left for London for two years and then returned to the Gold Coast in 1947. Nkrumah portrays his leaving by explaining the surrendered state of the colonial students mindset. They develop a fragmented mindset by focusing singularly on the problems raised by the great philosophers without focusing on the very real effect of colonial domination of which he was currently experiencing. As a philosophy student, he uses that subject as the basis for the descriptive motif. He refers to the abstract way in which the subject is addressed and the manner in which it is received, as if it is only training for proper ways in which to place statements in proper relationship while engaging in reflection. Of course this is done without any consideration given to the thought that early philosophers were purposeful in their applications of the skill of reflection. Even when they approached the universal while engaging in their reflective experiment, they began with the particular. The victims of colonial education were becoming experts in abstract universals disconnected from existence and complicit the continuation in their own, as well as their nation's oppression. Accordingly, Nkrumah expresses that his matriculation in America during this moment of the African American freedom struggle gave him the ability to recognize the utility of philosophy in his struggle against colonialism.[17]

The consequence of oppression in the form of alterity is communicated by Nkrumah in such a universal sense that it seems sensible and beneficial to think through his suggestions in terms of their application to blackness in other places, particularly in the United States. As the question is reframed from: what has alterity done to me; or what am I doing because of alterity? The complete range of answers to this question cannot possibly be addressed in this space; however, the focal point of Nkrumah's consideration on the matter will suffice. Within the text, the deliberate discussion of this subject falls under the title, "Society and Ideology." The core message of the section is grounded in the function of ideology within a society. Within Nkrumah's use, ideology helps to bind a society through the provision of the society's fundamental principles, its beliefs about the nature of human beings, and the type of society which must be be created for human beings.[18] This ideology must be pervasive in every existing social system within the society. Two or more ideologies cannot coexist peacefully. The dominant ideology constructs basic thoughts and morays, which also constructs the forms that all institutions must take. There is no successful dissent from the dominant ideology, for the members of a society obligate themselves to the dominant ideology. The dominant ideology in a society is successful when the members of the oppressed group, the other, believe that they are wrong or out of order when they think differently than their oppressor. This is so even when the dominant ideology calls for or leads to the destruction of the other. To say it plainly, one devastating effect of alterity or in this case blackness is that it causes many of those who are Black to believe that the ways of Black people must be destroyed. This includes the history, institutions, and cultural trappings, and in many ways the people themselves must also be destroyed.

ALTERITY AND SEGREGATION

How can a society have need of a group of people while at the same time convince that group and themselves that they are at best, ancillary and at worse, irrelevant? How can an ideology be used to convince oppressed people to be complicit in their destruction, whether ideologically or otherwise? To answer these questions in one word, segregation. To be Black in the United States was to be always already separated from humanity in the form of an assumed inherent flaw in one's humanity and character. The Black person was assumed not to be fully evolved or evolved differently than the white person, an imperfect evolution. An assumption of this nature is inherent in any notion of supremacy. Segregation as a state of being and its effects are best described by Howard Thurman in a 1965 text entitled, *The Luminous Darkness*: "The fact that the first twenty-three years of my life were spent in Florida and Georgia has left scars deep in my spirit and has rendered me terribly sensitive to the churning abyss separating white from Black."[19] Thurman suggests in the subtitle of the text, *A Personal Interpretation of the Anatomy of Segregation and the Ground of Hope,* that his intent is to discuss the components contained in the making of segregation and those of otherness. Thurman's description of alterity in the form of segregation negates the ability of the other to gain access to the very qualities which humanize because exterior to the community. What is also interesting is that according, to Thurman, the created world of otherness which develops in segregation creates two spheres of alterity. In each sphere, the other exterior to the sphere is not thought to be human in a way commensurate with the community interior to the sphere.[20] In spite of this dual alterity, the Black person knows that the conditions in which they are forced to exist are subpar. They believe the white person to be less than human because they have created the conditions in which they exist and the white person believes Black people to be less than human because they can exist under such conditions. Such conditions cause feelings of inferiority to overwhelm the person with a segregated status. "We were despised so long at last we despised ourselves."[21]

Community development is a necessary human characteristic and, as such, it is also a human right. The truth of this statement extends from the notion that there are two claims being put forward. The fact that humans are born into a community consisting of at least two members establishes the first claim; while the second claim requires that it be implicitly understood that all living things evolve and do so in such a manner as to increase the viability of life. To restrict community development restricts future possibilities, effectually restricting the viability of life, especially human life. As a Black person, there is an inherent right to be human, right? If so, then does the right to life, liberty, and the pursuit of happiness include a right to humanity? Thurman's work in this area, especially in this book, suggests that the proper consideration is not often given to where we individually and we as a group stand with respect to this conviction. To say that an individual has the right to be human is inclusive of several caveats, one being community development. It is not my intent to explore all the caveats in this text, but only to think deeply about the subject where Thurman finds it necessary to throw light on the matter.

Why would Thurman write such a book in 1965? In 1963, Thurman was in attendance at the March on Washington, where King was the featured speaker. From this experience, Thurman was moved to believe, as were many others, that this marked the beginning of new possibilities for Black Americans. However, Thurman correctly intuited that the nation was also on the verge of a crisis, aside from, but in concert with, the continuing constrictions caused by segregation. The adjudication of 1954 *Brown v. Board of Education* Supreme Court case, along with other factors, set in motion the realization among many Black people that an attitude of rejection, specifically of segregation, was necessary in order for the customs associated with segregation to pass. It was the horrible reactionary tactics of white people, especially in the South, which helped Thurman to see this new crisis. Thurman had this to say,

> The use of electric cattle prods, the turning of the full driving stream of water for the fighting of fires upon little children, defenseless girls, the dynamiting of a church resulting in the violent death of little children, ambushing of men in cold blood, the brutalizing of vulnerable women in the stark desolation of jail cells—these are deeds of men with their backs against the wall; they are at war. And the stakes: the established pattern that is fading away. There is no preparation in mind or heart or culture for relating to [Black people] outside of the segregated pattern.

This analysis offered by Thurman gets to the core of the connection between segregation and alterity brought on by the lack of the experience of humanity due to the forced reduction in contact with other humans. Accordingly, there can be no increase in humanity brought about by this reduction in contact with other humans and certainly not by the act of dehumanizing other humans.

In this type of created alterity, it becomes simple to believe that the experience of existing as other is the only means of existence, or that this type of existence and the accompanying essence is fundamental to their humanity, instead of being fundamental to their condition. All complications that accompany living in a fold or crevice caused by an artificially created wrinkle in the human experience becomes grafted into the culture and becomes replicated as if this is who they are as a fact of being rather than who they have become as fact of material reality. In this sense, those who have been oppressed through alterity began to believe that the created societal caricatures are true and fundamental. The oppressor comes to believe that they are just the opposite. Both are harmful. Much of the harm that exists is owing to the difficulty those affected have in simply engaging and disengaging from the behaviors brought about by the presence of alterity. Traveling can sometimes be effective in changing core beliefs one may hold about reality, but sometimes we simply move our bad beliefs to a different locale. These beliefs become the lens through which the world is perceived and all things are understood through this lens. Once anyone affected by this type of alterity, in the form of segregation, the individual and the community realizes their very ability to be human is being destroyed, it is then that they also realize that they must reject segregation at all cost.

The loss of humanity and the inherent necessity to reject segregation was central to Thurman's impetus for the text. His considerations on the matter stem from his fear that the value derived from the experience of being in community was irrevocably damaged through segregation.[22] Thurman was concerned that the longer the institution lasted, the farther distanced communities separated by segregation would grow. The final effect could be assumed to be a drastic reduction in the ability to treat anyone as human who is different than the community of which one is directly connected. Thurman points out that, "To experience oneself as a human being is to feel life moving through one and claiming one as a part of it."[23] While it is true that Thurman subscribed to a philosophical mysticism, the concept being put forth is not a mysterious one, at all. What Thurman intended to communicate was the process by which we know others to be human and the experience implicit in gaining such knowledge. In order to truly comprehend Thurman's intent, a simple framing of the process of experiencing is helpful. Being trained in the system of process thinker Alfred North Whitehead,[24] I find this way of framing useful on this matter. He denotes three means of experiencing: perception (sensory), imagination, and memory. Each are equally important but it is imagination that I want to bring to the fore. Imagination is required to make the move from knowing ourselves through our own experiences, based upon our perceptions and our memories or recollections. Without our imagination or when imagination has been damaged, which here can be loosely understood to be the cognitive activity necessary to move from perception to recognition, we simply cannot identify with the other. The fear for Thurman is that the ability to do this work of imagining gets damaged in just this manner through exposure to the segregative experience. We lose the very ability to see the other in our own image, the segregated and the segregationist.

ALTERITY AND RECOIL: FRAGMENTATION AS COMMUNAL EFFECT

In an environment where alterity is thought to ground human existence, one cannot simply assume that they are unaffected by the presence of alterity, especially alterity in the form of segregation. When it exists within the proximity of the individual or the community, regardless of their lack of participation in the experience of oppression or the act of oppressing, they are still affected. Fragmentation is the final result of alterity.[25] Between the period from 1896 through the 1970s, a legally segregated society arose in the aftermath of slavery, flourished for almost a century, but eventually met its legal demise. However, the legal demise of this segregated society did not correspond with the lived experience or the existential concerns of Black people. In the 1964 introduction to his book, *Why We Can't Wait*, Martin Luther King Jr. wrote, "Why does misery constantly haunt the Negro?"[26] This question implies the acknowledgment of the distance between the legal scene and lived experience of blackness. Segregation, or to use the more common nomenclature, Jim Crow, was kept on life support well beyond the 1954 *Brown v. Board of Education* legal victory for Thurgood Marshall and the NAACP. In this section, the thoughts of Martin Luther King Jr. and others will be used to explore what might be the lingering effect of Jim Crow or the measurement of its recoil on those within its proximity.

In order to perform this exploration, King's book *Where Do We Go from Here* will be used to frame my perspective on the topic. It is in this book that King centered the discussion around the notion that America is a community, despite any consensus of opinion. It is bound together by law, history, and material reality. However, as King demonstrates in the text, these markers do not necessarily override the racist impulses within the culture at large. As racist impulses also have their roots in the law, history, and material reality, such that the manner in which these form the machinations of the state, along with the cultural productions of the population, they provide little space for claims made by individuals of not being racist. The point here is that focusing on who is or who is not a racist is a lower concern than how the impulses formed by our proximity to a dehumanizing oppressive environment function to create the impulse to dehumanize others. For example, "historically" individuals are prone to distance themselves and their families from the ugly past of owning other human beings, but there are very few who can distance the same family from the effects of living in a slave-owning society. The more interesting philosophical question would be what moral quandaries do we face as a society resulting from our over exposure to oppression? And, to what human struggles have we, as a society proving to lack empathy? The implications from these types of societal assessments made King wrestle with core determinations about the nature of our society's development and the direction of our aim.

C. Vann Woodward begins his book *The Strange Career of Jim Crow* with the following connection, "The long experience of slavery in America left its mark on the posterity of both slave and master and influenced relations between them more than a century after the end of the old regime."[27] However, as stated earlier, the legal decline was inconsistent with the experiential reality. Oppressive court decisions occurring in 1857 and 1896 along with the infamous Hayes-Tilden Act of 1877 damaged future possibilities for the true experience of freedom by Black people, and these were not struck down until the 1954 *Brown* decision.[28] By comparison, other major actions made by either the United States congress or the nation's courts after 1954 were rather quick to follow. Nevertheless, because of the long, torturous span of time which the Jim Crow period covered, depraved attitudes of bigotry were allowed to stiffen, penetrating all constituent spaces and entities. The now-classic work on race by Michael Omi and Howard Winant *Racial Formation in the United States* shared this perspective, "From the very inception of the Republic to the present moment, race has been a profound determinant of one's political rights, one's location in the labor market, and indeed one's sense of 'identity.'"[29]

As more Black people moved from rural areas to cities, the national exposure to the depraved attitudes of American bigotry were demonstrated as being not only a Southern problem. Newark, Detroit, Chicago, and New York along with other major cities, were being exposed as sharing the same phenomenon. King recognized that the fallacious intent which created the empty rhetoric of the founding documents was in need of a new logic. The logic needed was one which could reconstruct the mindset of the average American, such that they thought in terms of what the documents should have meant for all humans present in the new American moment. No strict readings of these documents could be valid for King which limited the very humanity of any document readers.[30] Contemporary philosopher Greg Moses put it this way in his text *Revolution of Conscience: Martin Luther King, Jr. and the Philosopher of NonViolence*: "Another American Revolution . . . not exactly a return to where we were, but a journey toward where we ought to have been headed all along."[31] Moses finishes his thought on the matter by referencing American philosophy specifically, but his answer is relevant in broad terms to this scenario. He states that, "The pragmatic answer to this situation is not to moralize about the character or intent—either offensively or defensively—but to reconstruct habits so that subsequent consequences are none racists in their impact."[32]

King wrestled with a similar type of new logic which could lead to reconstruction in the final chapter of his last book *Where Do We Go from Here: Chaos or Community?* In this chapter, it was his understanding that the world population had grown to such a point that learning to live together was mandatory. If not, a fragmented nation and with the current proximity was not sustainable. Proximity made the world inherently one. The argument King put forward was that the very proximity of alterity, which was inherently an unequal manifestation of human existence, held severe consequences and even a recoil effect for the world. No longer could the world in general, and the United States in particular, sustain a dialectic of freedom, one Black and the other white, one rich and the other poor, or even one male and the other female. The fallout would affect all. This need to correct this was now clearly a moral problem. According to King, scientific progress was in abundance, but the nation and even the world was in moral decline. The moral decline had much to do with living in a space in which alterity was allowed to thrive, which in turn created a self-destructive attitude that the others in the world don't matter. King intimated that, "We have allowed the means by which we live to outdistance the ends for which we live." King made the connection between Du Bois's dictum, in the dawning of the twentieth century, concerning the problem of the color line, and America's continued struggle with the same hellhound at the close of the century. But he also pointed out that racism went hand in hand with economic exploitation. King saw that there was no opportunity to make the claims for capitalism being a superior economic system when there was continued support from America of racism and exploitation, at home and abroad. King stated that those from impoverished spaces at home and abroad would either be able to share in the blessings of Western scientific advancement or they would be motivated to form alliances aimed at Western destruction. King also realized that the reluctance to correct the disparity was not a resource problem, but simply a problem of human will. King laid the problem of the disparity in the world at the feet of the West because it was the Western powers who had been the former colonial masters and set the problems in motion, but were oblivious to the recoil effect of their actions because of their moral decay directly resulting from their proximity to alterity.

FREEDOM GAZING

Alterity is implicit in the act of freedom gazing particularly when applied to the experience of blackness. Freedom gazing as a perceptual framework within the experience of blackness and also within African American philosophy, as philosophy of the Black experience, bounds or gives shape to the thoughts or ideas regarding the condition of oppressed humans because of blackness. The importance of acknowledging the interconnection or confluence of alterity with freedom at this juncture is to serve as an explanatory function of the development of a separate discourse by those philosophizing about the Black experience, particularly by those who are Black. Within this discourse certain factors get conceptualized which are not considered or are outright dismissed when launching the philosophizing from other points of departure. The guiding question for this chapter, which was "what has my blackness done to me?," sets the stage for beginning the philosophical adventure from blackness as a point of departure. In order to do so, one must first contemplate the material reality of Black people along with their existential condition. Each of the thinkers explored in this chapter was intentional in centering the black experience while also taking up the topic of alterity in some mode.

There was a significant shift in the nature of what counted as the Black experience for the thinkers and their writings which were chosen for this chapter. *Consciencism* (Nkrumah) was written in 1964, *The Luminous Darkness* (Thurman) was written in 1965, and *Where Do We Go from Here* (King) was written in 1968. By the dates of their publication, social movements among the broader Black population both nationally and abroad had become widespread, motivated by more than a century of thinkers on the matter of the disconnected nature of black existence from freedom while also realizing the connectedness of the freedom struggle to economic mobility. After World War II and the *Brown v. Board* decision, along with increased American involvement in the Vietnam War, those within the communities were slowly beginning to additionally become aware of the worldwide effect of white oppression. Freedom gazing and the freedom gazer had to become concerned about other people's oppression with the realization that this concern set the bounds of their humanity. A lack of concern about oppression was also a lack of concern for their own humanity. In this sense, each thinker struggled with the essence of alterity particularly in the connection to Black humanity. In effect, freedom gazing was now becoming increasingly interchangeable with a type of Black humanocentric thought, meaning simply that many in the freedom struggle were coming to believe that the basic questions of their humanity to be consistent with and to inherently imply questions concerning their freedom.

ETHNIC REFLECTIVE CANON

Alain Locke wrote, "the high cost of prejudice, to which we had all but become accommodated, is now being compounded by the high price of integration. Together they add up to a capital levy [a drain on resources], and strain to the utmost on our artistic resources and our intellectual morale." For Locke, this loss of Black folk culture was equivalent to the loss of Black communal strivings for freedom.[33] Locke's statement is insightful in several respects. Jim Crow was faltering. However, with the demise of Jim Crow, there were numerous benefits; nevertheless, also came cracks in the lines of the enclosed nature of Black culture. Given this factor, there are some who would reject the assertion of certain works being constituent members of the ethnic reflective canon. In particular, the claim that the works of the ethnic reflective canon were being read and referenced mainly by Black people was losing its precision. Locke's point was that white Americans were beginning to read the works of Black thinkers and make comments on these works, and their comments were beginning to be referenced even by other Black thinkers. However, their place in the ethnic reflective canon continues to have validity because of the problems with which they grappled, the starting point from which many of them began their thoughts, and the serious manner in which they responded to works by other Black people from the past that many whites would have taken to be irrelevant. Also, while these works were on the periphery of white thought, they were central to Black thinking on these matters. An example of this would be Thurman's *Jesus and the Disinherited*. Few Black religious thinkers or otherwise, during the modern era, would have exempted this book from their reading list, owing to its importance within the previously described African American ethnic reflective canon.

NOTES

1. Howard Thurman, *Jesus and the Disinherited* (New York: Abingdon, 1949)
2. Mack H. Jones, *Knowledge, Power, and Black Politics: Collected Essays* (New York: SUNY, 2014).
3. William Barrett, *Irrational Man* (Garden City, NY: Doubleday, 1962), p. 4.
4. *Disciplinary Decadence*, p. 27.
5. Cesaire, *Discourse on Colonialism*, p. 8.
6. *Caste, Class, and Race*, xxxi.

7. Ibid., p. 153.
8. Ibid., p. 332.
9. Ibid., p. 546.
10. Refer to Michael E. Sawyer's *Africana Philosophy of Temporality: Homo Liminalis* (New York: Palgrave Macmillan, 2019).
11. *Luminous Darkness*, p. 94.
12. *Native Son*, p. 28.
13. Nkrumah's term.
14. This is to be understood in terms of the prescribed educative path.
15. *Philosophy of African American Studies*, p. 1.
16. Modern Ghana.
17. *Consciencism*, p. 5.
18. Ibid., p. 57.
19. *Luminous Darkness*, p. x.
20. Ibid., p. 3.
21. Ibid., p. 24.
22. Ibid., p. 98.
23. Ibid.
24. Whitehead, *The Function of Reason*.
25. Fragmentation here can be understood as acting individually or communally without giving any thought to how individual or communal acts affect or are disruptive to whole. It is not sustainable, in this sense, for individuals or communities to become alienated from the whole. A fragmented whole eventually breaks apart.
26. *Why We Can't Wait*, p. xii
27. *The Strange Career of Jim Crow*, p. 11.
28. Denote the legal decisions.
29. Michael Omi, and Howard Winant, *Racial Formation in the United States: From the 1960s to the 1980s* (New York: Routledge, 1991), p. 1.
30. Greg Moses, *Revolution of Conscience: Martin Luther King, Jr., and the Philosophy of Nonviolence*, "King's American Dream," 2015.
31. Ibid.
32. Ibid.
33. Alain Locke, 1952. "The High Price of Integration: A Review of the Literature of the Negro for 1951," *The Phylon*, 7; Anthony Sean Neal, https://1000wordphilosophy.com/2021/02/16/african-american-existentialism/.

Chapter 5

From Freedom to Fragmentation through Liberalism

If the modern era has ended, where are we now? In chapter 4, Martin Luther King Jr.'s book, *Where Do We Go from Here?*, was discussed Upon further reflection the title seems to necessitate asking the question, where are we now? Even if a debate were to ensue about some particular point that I have made within this text thus far, it seems that it would be difficult to disagree with the assertion that after slavery, Black people in America and Black thinkers more specifically, in the same grouping began to think of themselves and therefore about the nature of blackness in a different manner. By extension, it seems likewise, just as difficult to dispute that at a certain pattern within this manner of thinking came to an end along with the ending of legal segregation. In this concluding chapter, an obvious prerequisite I will address is the notion that some of the patterns of thought from this manner of thinking fell away and some remained. Identifying these contents while also attempting to locate the landing point after the moment of transition will be the focus of my aim in this final chapter.

Finding a point with which it can be said that here lies the location in time where the modern era came to an end and a new era arose from the ashes is a very difficult proposition. The difficulty arises from the improbability of offering something that could be put forward as a cause of this phenomenon. One suggestion taken from the point made above might be to determine the point at which certain patterns of thought began to fall away. However, this is very difficult because many of the ideas produced by the patterns of thought continued to hang on in perpetuity. By way of analogy, classical Greek society passed away but many of their ideas remain with us today. This loose analogy holds because many of the ideas, such as the meaning of blackness and how should Black people think about their oppression, which was developed during the modern era remain today. An example of this type of phenomenon would be the polarity that existed between Booker T. Washington and Richard

Wright on the question of forgiveness. Even today there exists the argument over where should Black people stand on this question of forgiveness.

The difficulty in locating this moment opens any discussion of the existence of such a moment to the epistemological question of what counts for certainty? However, accuracy of the location of such a moment is not so much my focus. The more important target here is the existence of the effect of such a moment on a large swath of Black thought as captured by Black social thinkers. If a certain constellation of temporal oriented phenomena can be identified as seemingly having a similar beginning point, then it is plausible that a new temporal moment has begun or at least that an old temporal moment has come to a halt. Basically, the identification of a new wide scale, shift in what can be attributed as being a constituent part of the Black experience would be an example of the type of temporal phenomenon of which I am referring. The phenomenon I will focus upon, the social network, was first discussed in chapter 2. As stated in that chapter, the Black social network, which was legally segregated, shaped and gave credibility to the existence of the modern era of the African American freedom struggle. It must also be remembered that during the modern era it was the connections with the common Black people that were actually striving for freedom from oppression, this is the common working-class people, that those thinkers within the network formed their most significant ties. Just as Du Bois, this is where those thinkers saw their work and these are the people who primarily read their work and took it seriously during their lifetime. When the modern era dissolved, this phenomenon slowly fell away.

The notion of a movement toward freedom made by a legally oppressed group of people that were once constitutionally in the bondage of chattel slavery is a radical one. However, one must keep this in tension with the troublesome existence of contravening ideas and strategic philosophies concerning what freedom would actually look like and what was the best direction to take for the achievement of such freedom. Basically, in spite of the ability for this group to have such a radical desire in terms of a flourishing existence, there was no existence of a consistent internal logic. Some were revolutionary in terms of strategy, but conservative in terms of their notion of freedom. Others were conservative in terms of strategy but revolutionary in terms of their notion of an ideal freedom. Still others were in the middle on both accords. For example, the strategy to integrate into the ongoing sociopolitical structure or any variation of being included into the existing sociopolitical structure with certain modifications made to facilitate such a widespread inclusion but without significant adjustments such as the repair of any past harm that would make those whole who had experienced a disinherited status was a conservative approach. But, one example of radical and even revolutionary strategy was the attempt to create a nation within a nation, such as the Republic of

New Africa, and along with this was the comparable notion of an ideal freedom which grounded the impetus of those whose effort formed the push for Black Studies programs.[1]

The notion of the different actors playing a role in the same movement regardless of their differing strategies or ideological commitments came together into a jazz-like dissonant melody because of the role that their desires and their commitment to some concept of freedom held. It was because of their desire for freedom which acted as a catalyst for the freedom aesthetic that they could bond and form a collective such as the Black community. However, around the time of the 1954 *Brown v. Board of Education* decision, fissures began to appear demonstrating the difficulty in holding such a community together. The differing strategies and levels of commitment to the goal of freedom began to obfuscate the path toward the achievement of any such aim as Black communal freedom. Several questions arose but seemed to go unspoken. Despite the unspoken nature of the questions, they were at the root of the differing strategic positions and the level of commitment. I will take up a few of these questions in this chapter, but certainly the questions that arose during this moment are not limited to the ones I reference here.

In this chapter, in an effort to conclude this book with the establishment of a concluding moment to the modern era, I have determined not to use the triad of thinkers scheme previously used in the other chapters, but instead I will opt for using a triad of concerns, first offered here in the form of questions, which will on one level offer space for the discussion of the splintered Black community that existed at the twilight of the modern era. While on the other hand, space will also be made available for this discussion to emerge into the concerns found in critical analyses of Black thinkers in this twilight moment in which they focused on what was blackness, or the Black experience, for the majority of Black people? I think it is also necessary to provide some assessment of the prevailing intellectual moment which ensued. The guiding questions for the triad of concerns I will use are as follows: Can there be a notion of Black freedom or freedom for Black people without some notion of the Black community? How has the growing class divide thwarted the struggle for freedom? Does holding on to the notion of being Black hinder forward progress?

In the title to this chapter, I use the words fragmentation and liberalism in the title. I think it is wise at this point to say something about my intended use of each, especially where I am deviating from common use. Fragmentation was used in my last book, but the goal there was to take Thurman's meaning and to extend from him but with a certain commitment to his standpoint. From Thurman's standpoint, the more important reference of fragmentation concerns its reference to the individual. In this sense, Thurman defined the term as the attempt by one to separate their outer action from their inner consciousness. An example of this usage would be to believe that violence against women is wrong while supporting a movement or cause which differs grossly on the matter. For Thurman, to be inconsistent in this manner predisposed the individual to a type of inconsistent nature limiting their potential. Accordingly, the intended use for the purpose of this book is more in line with a social framework, whereby the term can be taken to rise from the Marxist concept of alienation. Fragmentation, in this sense, is used to explain how class structure within a society breaks communal relations such that there is an absence of discourse and a reduce potential for social movement.[2] In either connotation provided here, fragmentation[3] is not seen as a positive, however the relevance of the social usage in this context is that it offers a frame from which to make a closer approximation of an interpretation of the breakdown within the Black community in the twilight of the modern era.

By way of distinction, liberalism focuses on personal autonomy. However, an important component of the discussion of liberalism in nations where it is fundamental to the political ideology, is who actually counts as a person, along with what rights are guaranteed to persons. A thorough breakdown on the matter is performed by Howard McGary in his coauthored text written with Bill Lawson. In this text, McGary demonstrates the problems liberalism poses in those societies that are ideologically linked to liberalism where there is a commitment to rights privileged over an idea of the good. This usually results in some group's rights being violated in the name of maintaining rights for others. In this section of McGary's book, which is labeled "Slavery, Paternalism, and Liberalism," he produces the demonstration of this occurrence by first explaining about the contradictions of the United States having a political ideology grounded in liberalism while simultaneously maintaining the institution of legalized slavery. The significance of McGary's thoughts on behalf of liberalism is that he reveals that too often liberalism, through its predilection toward exploitation, manages to explain these negative consequences by displaying a paternalistic attitude regarding those they exploit.

Freedom, equity, and consciousness[3] were constituent parts of the desired experience for those who were members of the Black community during the modern era. This can be easily shown through the causes of protests such as the Montgomery Bus Boycott, the Watts Uprising, and earlier campaigns against lynching. There is also an element of this desire present in the writings of the various individuals mentioned through this text. In particular, Du Bois, in his *The Souls of Black Folk*, unfolds the work in such a manner as to build the text in intensity in terms of forcing the reader into agreement that the people of which he is speaking not only desire these elements, but deserve them based upon their demonstrated humanity evidenced by the ending chapter, "Sorrow Songs." The organizations of which Black people developed had these constituent elements as their aim. Organizations such as the American Negro Academy, the NAACP, the Pullman Porters Union, and the SCLC made this very apparent in the nature of their activities. After 1965, which was the year that Malcolm X died, there is a significant turn by Black Americans to identify with the struggles for these constituent elements by other Black people around the world. The first noticeable evidence of this was the rejection of the term Negro for the term Black spelled with a capital "B" as they took it to refer to a specific group of people identified by a set of cultural practices and history. Organizations such as the Black Arts Movement and the Black Panther Party were created. This shift had an effect internationally also. In South Africa, the Black Consciousness Movement founded by Stephen Bantu Biko was also influenced by this more international turn in the United States as well as other international currents.[4]

In order to properly focus this final chapter, while moving swiftly toward a conclusion, it is necessary to say something about my own inspiration to enter into academia in general and philosophy more specifically. In 1996, I heard an interview by Charlie Rose with Cornel West and Henry Louis Gates Jr., "The Future of the Race." The interview was concerning the book coauthored by Gates and West, which had the same title. At the time, I did not have the interpretive skills I have today and I was just excited to see two Black people on television delivering their elocution in such a profound style. This event awoke in me a fire inspiring me to get my doctorate and to attempt to become a professor. I felt as if I was answering their call to be the future of the race. Later, while in graduate school, I came across the writings of Adolph Reed Jr., and it was these writings that helped me to put into perspective the earlier interview and subsequent book, which I purchased soon after seeing the interview.

It was in the writings of these three scholars that I found my research agenda. I wanted to understand in some deep and profound way what had become of what my parents called the movement. Certainly, there had been a movement. So many adults with whom I came into contact spoke about it so vividly. Nevertheless, by the eighties whatever was the movement was just a fizzle and by nineties there was nothing radical left of the Black side of town. It had become the "hood." How had this happened right before my eyes? Without detailing much more of my personal experience, here I will pivot in order to throw light upon how this book in a meaningful way, exposes the reality modern era, grapples with some of the existential concerns philosophically, and in this points to a determination about its ideological demise. To capture more fully a notion of the demise of the movement beyond the ideological would require a much longer effort and a retelling of narratives which have already been reported by others. My concern here was only why did a certain type of thought come to an end? In other words, what discontinued the ideological struggle for freedom, particularly among the intelligentsia?

CAN THERE BE A NOTION OF FREEDOM FOR BLACK PEOPLE WITHOUT A NOTION OF THE BLACK COMMUNITY?

A more philosophical question might be posed: Is there any meaningful connection between freedom and community for an oppressed group of people? After slavery, the recognition that Black people, particularly in the South, needed to band together to form communities of protection was a foregone conclusion. Black codes, the convict lease–apprenticeship program and the rise of sundown towns were just a few of the oppressive inventions whites instituted in order that Black people would struggle to gain any notion of a flourishing existence. However, soon came those who felt that Black communities and organizations banding together because of their experience as Black people was reductive and would limit the power of any organization aimed at progress. Three thinkers in particular, Abram Harris, E. Franklin Frazier, and Ralph Bunche, were adamant about this point. Ralph Bunche would go as far as to make a comparison between race-based organizations and Hitler by saying, "They, like Hitler, even though for different reasons, think that all that is not race in this world is trash."[5] Bunche was a political scientist, Frazier was a sociologist, and Harris was economist. All three were scholars at Howard University, and all three were considered to have radical ideas. But, what is of note here is they each thought that because of The New Deal, there was the possibility to make the shift from race concerns first toward the consideration of class concerns as a mode and method of reenvisioning American society. Absent the space for a robust description of their ideas and ideological transformation with time, it suffices to say that the most salient commitment each of these thinkers maintains is their belief that race, and to be more exact, racism could be overcome through a focus on class. Accordingly, they each worked from the position of a Jamesian pragmatism,[6] a position which arose from a type of practical mindset. However, this mindset was certainly in contention with the average Black person of their time.[7] This trend of a division between the Black intelligentsia and the common Black person did not end with these three and effectively removed most Black scholars from the conversation of a Black communal freedom, whether they fully agreed with these three or not. Their active participation, whether scholarly or otherwise, became distant from the goals of common Black people as they pertained to freedom struggle. The removal of the Black intelligentsia from the active throes of the struggle for freedom was to become a heavy and possibly fatal blow.

One point of interest is that the burgeoning international counterpart to the Black struggle for freedom in America began to focus more on Black consciousness and decolonization, a type of racial separation. This point is interesting because this movement took as its starting point the beginnings of Negritude thought and their weaving together of ideas that arose during the early moments of the struggle for freedom in America, such as the Harlem Renaissance moment. But, by 1957, the year of Ghanian independence led by Kwame Nkrumah, it became clear that decolonization was the way to forward progress. Other resistance movements based on these ideas and a type of organizing on the basis of Africanity produce new scholar/revolutionary leaders such as Amilcar Cabral and Stephen Biko. In spite of both being influenced by Marxist thought, they each saw ineffective consequences of not organizing around cultural groupings. They were not against concepts such as the Marxist slogans, "All men are brethren," or "Workers of the world unite."[8] However, they also realized the deep psychosocial effect that racism had on white people and Black people alike, making it difficult to form bonds quickly, creating a human front against existential crisis created by colonization. I say white people and Black people suffered from this effect, but to be clear, it was white people who had amassed the unchecked and unconscionable power to act on it. White people in the form of national governments had the force of large national militaries and economies all geared toward protecting a certain way of life.

HOW HAS THE GROWING CLASS DIVIDE THWARTED THE STRUGGLE FOR FREEDOM?

To expose what I am referencing in my usage of class divide, the experiences of Cornel West and Henry Louis Gates Jr. in the early 1970s will be placed into perspective by also bringing to the fore the experiences of common Black people for whom the movement of Blacks struggling for freedom was referencing around the same time period. Much of this analysis will be performed in consideration of the text by Harold Cruse, *The Crisis of the Negro Intellectual*.[9] In the space allotted to Gates, he uses much of it to reflect upon his undergraduate experience at Yale, while West begins his portion with a critique of Du Bois. Before I begin to assess and critique any of their reflections in this section, the question must be asked, to whom are they writing and why? This question gets to the crux of what Cruse would refer to as a rootless class, basically having no ideological allegiance to any community, having been produced by one community but funded by another. An assessment of their aim is made by Adolph Reed in his book *Class Notes*.[10] In this text, Reed's chapter entitled, "What Are the Drums Saying Booker,"[11] makes a comparison between the "bearer" or servant for a white group safari in an old movie he was referencing and the precarious Black intellectual. Reed refers to the type of Black intellectual such as Gates and West, which he calls by name,[12] as a freelance race spokesman. Accordingly, Booker T. Washington is seen by Reed to be their precursor. Reed certainly does not neglect to identify the existence of other Black intellectuals both in the academy and out who attempt to counter Washington's position. However, the point here, and Reed's point to a certain extent, is that during Washington's day only Washington, and Frederick Douglass before him, had his type of prominence. However, much has changed today in terms of the placement of Black intellectuals in elite spaces and the ability of these spaces to readily provide the funding necessary to become the "Racial Voice accountable to no clearly identifiable constituency among the spoken for."[13]

In the first line from the section titled, "The Timorous Tenth," Gates specifically makes reference to the growing distance between the poor Blacks and more wealthier ones. Correspondingly, this also happened to be 1973, the year Gates graduated from college. The reporting by Gates of the highs and lows of the years he spent at Yale is somewhat enriching, but the present aim is more to explore a portion of his personal narrative, creating a level of understanding about his mindset, as an example of the developing intelligentsia. Two things immediately come to the fore and are perceptible throughout the section written by Gates. First, Gates is extremely proud of the excellent education he received. For that matter, there is absolutely no reason Gates or anyone else with the same education, should not be proud of an excellent formal education in a world in which formal education creates so many other opportunities. There is more that could be written about this moment in Gates's life; however, I do not wish to write anything that might seemingly be dismissive of education at the expense of deterring someone from pursuing their own education. Secondly, and the more interesting philosophical question, is that apparently, in the estimation of Gates, there are winners and losers. He clearly believes that he has won at life, and anything he does for the benefit of Black people is extra. It seems that Gates attaches no communal moral imperative to his station in life. I think his sentiment on the matter can be garnered from the following, "But I was fortunate; I loved this place. I loved the library and the seminars, I loved talking to the professors. . . . And I, like Tar Baby, would tell myself I had won."[14]

As stated earlier, West began his portion with an extended critique of Du Bois. While doing so, in sheer Du Boisian style, he managed to extend Du Bois's concepts into an expanded version of the former ethnographic style. Through his performance of this expansion, West paints himself and others, those similarly situated as him, into Du Bois's frame, while using the Victorian-styled Talented Tenth argument as a veneer for an underlying radical notion of liberalism as I defined it above. This is evidenced in his ending decree, "For those of us who stand on his broad shoulders, let us begin where he ended." Opposite from Gates, West does seem to feel a communal moral imperative; however, unlike Gates, the presence of this imperative dims his way forward and robs him of the ability to take pride in being among the elite. It seems that he assumes the self-loathing of the Talented Tenth can be assuaged through staying on the battlefield without actually affecting change. One thing is for certain, he does not believe that his own efforts will affect significant change as noted in the following, "the significant efforts of the Black Talented Tenth alone in the twenty-first century will be woefully inadequate and thoroughly frustrating."

In both segments, it is clear that West and Gates are of the belief that the modern era of the freedom struggle was gone by their college days, and truly gone for good because of a nearly insurmountable class divide. Gates's words on the matter are telling, "No longer could we be said to be the organic community we seemed to be when King had his day at the Lincoln Memorial." And likewise, it is the absence of words denoting their acknowledgment of an ongoing freedom movement. Each of these men exposes the difficulty that the newly minted Talented Tenth and the poor and unfortunate majority in the Black community has in forming a unified force ready to struggle for a flourishing existence for all.

DOES HOLDING ON TO A NOTION OF THE BLACK COMMUNITY HINDER FORWARD PROGRESS?

In light of Gates's direct statements on the matter of the discontinued existence of a Black community, perhaps a reframing of this question in a more philosophical mode should be as such, is there any value in thinking through the perceptual lens of a "Black community?" Although many African American scholars began to disperse from the movement, choosing instead to focus on their career, the struggle for freedom would take another turn and possibly a final turn in 1966. This final turn in many ways would act as a litmus test, separating those who were for peace, from the rebels and from the revolutionaries. Gates refers to this sort of litmus test when he discusses not feeling Black enough. His statement about this particular feeling could be nuanced to be understood as being Black enough as equivalent to being committed enough to the struggles that the average Black person encounters when trying to live a life that flourishes. In my first book *Common Ground*, to explain fully this notion using the most common wording of the notion by Black people, I employed the term consciousness.[15] Many Black people would simply refer to the individual's level of consciousness and not raise the question of them being Black enough. In 1966, the year of the founding of the Black Panther Party for Self Defense, they set as their major goal to raise the consciousness of the people. What did this mean? It meant to inform the Black people of the real nature of the Black experience in America. They felt that once the people became aware of their experience or once they became conscious, then the people themselves would bring about revolution. This revolution would call for a fundamental shift or reconstituting of the basic nature of human existence in relationship to their government. Accordingly, they called for "All Power to All the People."[16]

Community, for the Black Panther Party and their main theoretician, Huey Newton, was necessary for revolution. For many, especially the poor, the freedom struggle was fundamentally about causing a revolutionary change in American society. Without community, there can be rebellion but not revolution as stated in the first chapter. Revolution was necessary, in their understanding, because the the United States had breached a fundamental code of humanity through oppression and exploitation. The representative democratic government coupled with capitalism would always oppress in order to continue in the oppression of the underclass. The value of thinking in terms of a Black community was that it allowed Black people to see that along with poor whites, they formed the underclass. It also allowed Black people to focus on the experience of blackness in general, instead of some particular experience. Liberalism created a lens in which the individual counted everything as good as long as their personal success was achieved. The good in this sense is thought to be their individual success. The liberal may feel that everyone has the same chances or that life is precarious for everyone. However, liberality does not usually take into account the system itself put them in direct competition with other members of their community. They typically would place the blame on bad actors within the system, disregarding the fact that the success of the few is predicated on the failure of a great number of people. This was a point of stress for the Panthers. Just as Du Bois had, they wanted the people to see that phenomenon which they may have taken to be cultural problems or problems inherent to Black skin were really baked into the system for anyone in the lower class. And, that the solution to these kinds of problems were necessarily a social one, beginning at the communal level. Therefore, the value in thinking through the lens of Black community provides a clearer picture of reality and a clearer path to a solution.

CONCLUSION: SOME RESIGNED TO DESPAIR AND OTHERS TO FRAGMENTATION {ASSESSMENT AND CRITIQUE}

Struggle in the face of an existential crisis sometimes leads to despair; however, rejection of a social struggle by way of individualism leads to fragmentation of community, and also leads personal fragmentation. The modern era ended in both despair and fragmentation, and it is in this condition that Black people seemingly have remained. More faith was be placed into electoral politics. Hope in the success of a resistance movement which would bring about freedom, and equity, for all was slowly being replaced by hope for tolerance and reform.[17] The Panthers, along with other revolutionary-minded organizations, put forth an incredible effort to raise the consciousness of the people and to resist the oppressive exploitative forces against them, but the communal bonds among Black people were becoming fragile. Even within the Panther organization, infiltration by governmental forces began to cause conflict and strife. Resistance movements require endurance. Major rifts within the organization left the Panthers as a shell of itself while splinter groups such as the Black Liberation Army formed, but were unsuccessful in amassing wide support.[18] Prison resistance campaigns led by George Jackson resulted in his later being murdered by prison guards. Veterans of the Vietnam War returned home to decimated communities; many veterans suffered from drug addiction, alcoholism, and PTSD. Whereas, their counterparts, those who attended college and not war, those looking to take part in some of the greatest material gains seen by Black people in the United States ever, while they may have pragmatically given up on freedom, they found a substitute with which they learned to live.

In the Adolph Reed book, *The Jesse Jackson Phenomenon: The Crisis of Purpose in Afro-American Politics*, Reed gives three conditions which limit the ability of Black leadership's hope to have real political power.[19] The third of these I find to be most significant and it is in line with my assessment of the demise of the modern era. Reed wrote, "Integration of Black elites into the growth calculus, as I have argued, has opened opportunities for upwardly mobile Blacks—thereby segmenting the Black population economically into a relatively secure stratum at one end and dispossessed, option-less component at the other."[20] The problem with this, as Reed points out, is that the goals of each group have become distanced and incongruent. The goals of the upwardly mobile are: (a) affirmative action (b) high-status job appointments (c) specification of set-asides for minority contractors.[21] Angela Davis put it this way: "redress through electoral channels is the liberal's panacea."[22] However, in some ways, it seems that at the basis of American education, since integration at least, was the goal of making liberal-minded Americans, people who would no longer struggle to be free. And based upon my analysis of the modern era of the freedom struggle by Black people in the United States, grounded in the earlier writings of Adolph Reed and others, but gazing upon what I consider to be the radical liberalism of Gates, West, and others, the success of American education is crushing if not mentally, certainly physically.

NOTES

1. This is not to imply that in every Black Studies program today their current iterations have maintained an integrity in their commitment their founding ideas.

2. Alvin Gould, *Against Fragmentation* (Oxford: Oxford, 1985), p. 266.

3. Consciousness should be understood as knowledge of self, which in this context also implies the knowledge of one's history in conjunction with the knowledge of one's situation in life.

4. "Biko and the other founders of the Black Consciousness Movement in South Africa were inspired by a global moment of Black self-assertion and the works of a range of radical writers of the time. Among them were Frantz Fanon's *Black Skin, White Masks* and *The Wretched of the Earth*, Aimé Césaire's *Discourse on Colonialism*, John Mbiti's *Introduction to African Religions*, Eldridge Cleaver's *Soul on Ice*, C.L.R. James's *The Black Jacobins*, Stokely Carmichael and Charles Hamilton's *Black Power: The Politics of Liberation*, and *The Autobiography of Malcom X*. Key concepts and ideas were triggered by thinkers such as Charles Hamilton, James Cone, Cheikh Anta Diop, David Diop, Léopold Senghor, and Kenneth Kaunda as well as frameworks such as négritude and African humanism. Further stimulus flowed from the U.S. Civil Rights Movement of the late 1950s and 1960s, such as the Black Panther Party and the Montgomery Bus Boycott of 1955." https://mronline.org/2021/09/15/black-community-programmes-the-practical-manifestation-of-black-consciousness-philosophy/#:~:text=This%20dossier%20focuses%20on%20the%20Black%20Community%20Programmes,give%20Black%20people%20the%20power%20to%20become%20self-reliant.

5. Holloway, *Confronting the Veil*, p. 157.

6. i.e., Booker T. Washington.

7. Holloway, *Confronting the Veil*, pp. 197–198.

8. Communist Manifesto.

9. Harold Cruse, *The Crisis of the Negro Intellectual* (New York: New York Review Book, 2005), pp. 451–452.

10. Reed, *Class Notes*.

11. Ibid., pp. 77–90.

12. Ibid., p. 77.

13. Ibid., p. 79.

14. Henry Louis Gates and Cornel West. *The Future of the Race* (New York: Vintage Books, 1997), pp. 50–51

15. Neal, *Common Ground*, p. 1.

16. Ibid., p. 98.

17. Adolph L. Reed, *The Jesse Jackson Phenomenon: The Crisis of Purpose in Afro-American Politics* (New Haven: Yale University Press, 1986); Adolph L. Reed, *Class Notes: Posing As Politics and Other Thoughts on the American Scene*, 2001.

18. 1126840-000—157-HQ-10555-Bulky1359—Section 1. n.d. MS Black Liberation Army and the Program of Armed Struggle: The Black Liberation Army Collection 157 - 10555 - 74. Federal Bureau of Investigation Library. Archives

Unbound, link.gale.com/apps/doc/SC5104328342/GDSC?u=mag_u_msu&sid=GDSC&xid=58c23891&pg=2. Accessed 27 Jan. 2021.

19. Adolph L. Reed, *The Jesse Jackson Phenomenon: The Crisis of Purpose in Afro-American Politics* (New Haven: Yale University Press, 1986), p. 63.

20. Ibid.

21. Ibid., p. 65.

22. Angela Davis "Political Prisoners, Prisons, and Black Liberation" (1971).

Bibliography

Appiah, Anthony. *Lines of Descent: W. E. B. Du Bois and the Emergence of Identity.* Cambridge, MA: Harvard University Press, 2014.

Brisbane, Robert H. *The Black Vanguard: Origins of the Negro Social Revolution, 1900–1960.* Ann Arbor:, 1985.

Carter, Jacoby Adeshei. *African American Contributions to the Americas' Cultures.* New York: Palgrave Macmillan, 2016.

Chandler, Nahum Dimitri. *X—the Problem of the Negro as a Problem for Thought.* New York: Fordham University Press, 2014.

Cooper, Anna J. *A Voice from the South: By a Black Woman of the South.* Mineola, NY: Dover Publications, 2017.

Cox, Oliver Cromwell. *Caste, Class, and Race: A Study in Social Dynamics.* London: Forgotten Books, 2018.

Davis, Angela Y. *Freedom is a Constant Struggle.* New York: Penguin Books, 2021.

Descartes, René, Tom Griffith, and John Veitch. *Discourse on Method; Meditations on the First Philosophy; The Principles of Philosophy.* Indianapolis, IN: Hackett Publishing, 2004.

Du Bois, W. E. B. *Du Bois' Writings.* New York: The Library of America, 1995.

Du Bois, William E. B., and Isabel Eaton. *The Philadelphia Negro: A Social Study, with a New Introduction by Elijah Anderson.* Philadelphia: University of Pennsylvania Press, 1995.

Du Bois, William Edward Burghardt. *The Autobiography of W. E. B. Du Bois: A Soliloquy on Viewing My Life from the Last Decade of Its First Century.* New York: International Publications, 1971.

Du Bois, W. E. B. *Darkwater: Voices from within the Veil.* Mineola, NY: Dover, 1999.

Ellison, Ralph. *Shadow and Act.* New York: Random House, 1995.

Eze, Emmanuel Chukwudi. *Race and the Enlightenment: A Reader.* Malden, MA: Blackwell, 2009.

Ferris, William Henry. *The African Abroad: Or, His Evolution in Western Civilization, Tracing His Development Under Caucasian Milieu.* New York: Johnson Reprint Corp., 1968.

Gaines, Kevin Kelly. *Uplifting the Race: Black Middle-Class Ideology in the Era of the "New Negro," 1890–1935.* Chapel Hill: University of North Carolina Press, 1991.

Gates, Henry Louis, and Cornel West. *The Future of the Race.* New York: Vintage Books, 1997.

Glaude, Eddie S. *Begin Again.* New York: Penguin Random House, 2020.

Gooding-Williams, Robert. *In the Shadow of Du Bois: Afro-Modern Political Thought in America.* Cambridge, MA: Harvard University Press, 2011.

Hall, Stuart. *The Fateful Triangle: Race, Ethnicity, Nation.* Cambridge, MA: Harvard University Press, 2012.

Harrison, Hubert H., and Jeffrey B. Perry. *A Hubert Harrison Reader.* Middletown, CT: Wesleyan University Press, 2001.

Harrison, Hubert H., and Jeffrey Babcock Perry. *When Africa Awakes: The "Inside Story" of the Stirrings and Strivings of the New Negro in the Western World.* Halethorpe, MD: Black Classic Press, 2015.

Hoffer, Williamjames Hull. *Plessy V. Ferguson: Race and Inequality in Jim Crow America.* Lawrence, KS: University Press of Kansas, 2012. https://www.npr.org/2017/04/26/524744989/when-la-erupted-in-anger-a-look-back-at-the-rodney-king-riots

Jones, Mack H. *Knowledge, Power, and Black Politics: Collected Essays.* New York: SUNY Press, 2014.

Kadushin, Charles. *Understanding Social Networks: Theories, Concepts and Findings.* Oxford: Oxford University Press, 2018.

Kilson, Martin. *Transformation of the African American Intelligentsia, 1880–2012.* Cambridge: Harvard University Press, 2014.

Lawson, Bill E., and Frank M. Kirkland. *Frederick Douglass, A Critical Reader.* Malden, MA: Blackwell, 1999.

MacGary, Howard, and Bill E. Lawson. *Between Slavery and Freedom: Philosophy and American Slavery.* Bloomington: Indiana University Press, 1995.

Marcus Garvey, author, Robert A. Hill and Barbara Bair (eds), *The Marcus Garvey and Universal Negro Improvement Association Papers,* Vol. VII: November 1927–August 1940; p. 791.

Mills, Charles W. *Blackness Visible: Essays on Philosophy and Race.* Ithaca, NY: Cornell University Press, 2015.

Morris, Aldon. *Scholar Denied: W. E. B. Du Bois and the Birth of Modern Sociology.* Oakland: University of California Press, 2017.

Omi, Michael, and Howard Winant. *Racial Formation in the United States: From the 1960s to the 1980s.* New York: Routledge, 1991.

Patterson, Orlando. *Freedom.* New York: Basic Books, 1991.

Patterson, Orlando. *Slavery and Social Death: A Comparative Study.* Cambridge: Harvard University Press, 2018.

Perry, Jeffrey B. *Hubert Harrison: the Struggle for Equality, 1918–1927.* New York: Columbia University Press, 2021.

Perry, Jeffrey B. *Hubert Harrison: The Voice of Harlem Radicalism, 1883–1918.* New York: Columbia University Press, 2011.

Rabaka, Reiland. *W.E.B. Du Bois and the Problems of the Twenty-First Century: An Essay on Africana Critical Theory*. Lanham, MD: Lexington Books, 2008.

Reed Jr., Adolph. *Class Notes Posing As Politics and Other Thoughts on the American Scene*. La Vergne: The New Press, 2021.

Reed, Adolph L. *Fabianism and the Color Line: W.E.B. Du Bois and American Political Thought in Black and White*. New York: Oxford University Press, 1997.

Reed, Adolph L. *Stirrings in the Jug: Black Politics in the Post-Segregation Era*. Minneapolis: University of Minnesota Press, 1999.

Reed, Adolph L. *The Jesse Jackson Phenomenon: The Crisis of Purpose in Afro-American Politics*. New Haven: Yale University Press, 1986.

Reed, Adolph, Kenneth W. Warren, Madhu Dubey, William P. Jones, Michele Mitchell, Touré F. Reed, Dean E. Robinson, Preston H. Smith, and Judith Stein. *Renewing Black Intellectual History: The Ideological and Material Foundations of African American Thought*. New York: Routledge, 2015.

Robeson, Paul, and Lloyd L. Brown. *Here I Stand*. Boston: Beacon Press, 1971.

Simmel, Georg, and Kurt H. Wolff. *The Sociology of Georg Simmel*. New York: Free Press, 1964.

Smith, Edward L. "Prehension: A Process Version of Friedrich Schleiermacher's Theory of the Feeling of Absolute Dependence of God." Ann Arbor, Mich: UMI Dissertation Services, 1998.

Stewart, Jeffrey C. *The New Negro: The Life of Alain Locke*. 2020.

Thurman, Howard. *Jesus and the Disinherited*. 2022.

Wells-Barnett, Ida B., Henry Louis Gates, and Mia Bay. *The Light of Truth: Writings of an Anti-Lynching Crusader*. 2014.

Zamir, Shamoon. *Dark Voices: W. E. B. Du Bois and American Thought, 1888–1903*. Chicago: University of Chicago Press, 1997.

Index

accommodationism, 62–63
The Acorn (journal), 21
actual occasion, notion of, 7, 43n2
Africa: Hegel view of, 32, 59; Negritude movement and, 62; self-definition and, 16
The African Abroad (Ferris), 58, 62
African American culture: African diaspora influence on, 70; freedom gazing and, 7; struggle for freedom and, 47
African American freedom movement, 68; modern era of, x, xiin1
African American freedom struggle, 22, 41, 78; African diaspora and, 70; contributionism and, 60; modern era of, 2, 15; social networks and, 90
African American philosophy, xi, 1, 68; blindspots in, 69; goals of, 22
African American Studies, xi, 68
Africana Studies, 68
African diaspora, ix, 2; African American culture influenced by, 70; immigration to United States by, 16; shift in consciousness in, 69–70
Afro-pessimism, 59
Age of Enlightenment, 30, 31
alienation, 92

alterity, 69; Blackness and, 74–79; ethnic reflective canon and, 86; freedom gazing and, 85; negritude resisting, 62; racial antagonism and, 71–72; recoil and, 82–84; segregation and, 79–82
American Negro Academy (ANA), 49, 51, 52, 67, 93
Amo, Anton Wilhelm, 31
ANA. *See* American Negro Academy
anticolonial literature, 70
Apartheid, 38
"Apology" (Du Bois), 38
"Appeal" (Walker), 39
Appiah, Anthony, 44n22
Aristotle, 30, 31, 33
Atlanta Compromise, 33, 48, 49, 51
Atlanta Cotton Exposition, 48
Atlanta University, 52

Baker, Houston A., Jr., 16
Baker, Thomas Nelson, 33, 34
Baldwin, James, 3
Being, 34
being Black, experiential moment and, 25
beingness, 16, xiin1
Biko, Stephen Bantu, 93, 95, 100n4
Black Arts Movement, 93

The Black Atlantic (Gilroy), 16, 17
Black Atlantic culture, 17
Black beingness, 16
Black (Revolutionary) Christian tradition, 16
Black Codes, 49
Black community, 91; catalysts of changes in, 69; freedom and, 94–95; progress and notion of, 97–98
Black consciousness, 11, 95
Black Consciousness Movement, 93, 100n4
Black ethnically reflective thinkers, 8
Black Experience, xi, 15–18; philosophy of, 22; thought about, 11
Black humanity, value as freedom in, 47–52
Black Intelligentsia, 7
Black Liberation Army, 99
Black Nationalism, viii
Blackness, 2; alterity and, 74–79; color line and, 35; Du Bois on meaning of, 8, 21; ethnic reflective canon and, 4; experience of, 21; experiential moment of, 25; meaning of, 22; modern era meaning of, 15; temporal-spatial conditions and, 25
Black Panther Party, 93, 98, 99
Black people: as freedom gazers, 37; legal status of, 35–36, 44n21; nonacceptance of humanity of, 28; studying at Sorbonne, 62; on television, 93; violence and exploitation of, 40
Black Phenomenology, xiin1
Black Skin, White Mask (Fanon), 3, 73
Black Studies, 3, 68, 91
The Black Vanguard (Brisbane), 15
blues, 73
Blues, Ideology, and Afro-American Literature (Baker), 16
Blues People (Jones), 3
body, 34
Brisbane, Robert Hughes, 15, 16
British Royal Society, 32

Brown, Sterling, 62
Browne, Robert T., 51
Brown v. Board of Education, 80, 82, 85, 91
"brute" concept, 31
Bunche, Ralph, 94

Cabral, Amilcar, 95
Calypso, 73
capitalism, 84; oppression and, 98; racial exploitation and race prejudice and, 72; war and, 71
Cassirer, Ernst, 35
Caste, Class, and Race (Cox), 70
Catlett, Elizabeth, 12–13
Césaire, Aimé, 3, 63
chattel slavery, 32, 90
chicken theft, 55–56
civilization, 53
Civil Rights Era, xi
Civil Rights Movement, 67, 100n4
Civil War, constitutional amendments after, 49
class bias, 54
class divisions: political-class wars and, 71, 72; racial, vii; struggle for freedom and, 95–97
Class Notes (Reed), 96
cognition, 23
color line, 35
common good, 13
community development, 40, 42, 79–80; consciousness and, 25
Conscienticism (Nkrumah), 77, 85
consciousness, vii, 92; awakening, 60; community development and, 25; development of, 22; experiential moments and, 23–24; social transformation and, 25
contributionism, 60
"The Contribution of Race to Culture" (Locke), 53, 55
Cooper, Ana Julia, 35, 40, 42, 47
Cox, Oliver Cromwell, 70–73

The Crisis of the Negro Intellectual (Cruse), 95
"Criteria for Negro Art" (Du Bois), 57
Crummell, Alexander, 35, 48, 50–52, 61
Cruse, Harold, 95
Cullen, Countee, 4, 18n6, 62
culture: Black Atlantic, 17; race and, 53, 55. *See also* African American culture
Cusanus, Nicholas, 35

Davis, Angela, 12, 99
death, slavery as, 1
Declaration of Independence, 16, 27, 32
decolonization, 70, 95
dehumanization, 80–82; knowing self as human and, 6–7; slavery and, 6–7
Delany, Martin, 35
Descartes, Rene, 23, 31, 33–34, 51
Dewey, John, 43n2
dialectical idealism, 58–59
Discourse on Colonialism (Césaire), 3
Discourse on Methods (Descartes), 31
Douglass, Frederick, 11–12, 35, 40, 96
Du Bois, W. E. B., xi, 2–4, 42, 47, 51, 52, 92, xiin1; on art as propaganda, 57; on Black Intelligentsia, 7; as exemplar, 21–39; existential crisis of, 27–35, 72; experiential moment and, 25–27; Freedom Gazing and, 36–39; as integrationist, 63; on legal status of Black people, 36; on meaning of blackness, 8, 21; notion of resisting and rejecting used by, 6; race conceptions and, 44n22; scholar activist idea of, 35, 40, 61; social connections, 41; talented tenth idea, 58; turn towards scholar and activist, 29; West critique of, 95, 96–97
duration, 43n2
Dusk of Dawn (Du Bois), 26, 27, 38, 72

"Education and the Race" (Harrison), 61
Ellison, Ralph, 18
the Enlightenment, 30–33

equity, 92
essentialism, 18
"The ethical significance of the connection between mind and body" (Baker, T. N.), 33
ethnic reflective canon, 3, 4–7, 39–41, 48; alterity and, 86; New Negro thinkers and, 62–64
existential crisis, 99
existentialist philosophy, 30, 62, 63, 73
experience: knowledge of, 23; lived, 43n2; means of, 81
experiential moment, 22, 23–27, 73
"The Fact of Blackness" (Fanon), 74

Fanon, Frantz, 3, 73, 74
feelings, 5
Ferris, William H., 47, 58–63
first migration, 49
fragmentation, 82–84, 87n25, 91, 99
Francis of Assisi (Saint), 52
Frazier, E. Franklin, 94
freedom, vii, 91, 92, xiin1; Black community and, 94–95; class divide and struggle for, 95–97; mapping movement and, 10–11; as movement, 10; movement towards, 90; phenomena denoted by, 6; struggle and, 1, 2, 10, 48; theoretical, 39; value as, 47–52
freedom gazing, 7–9, 35–40, 43n14, 48; alterity and, 85; ethnic reflective canon and, 39; New Negro thinkers and, 60–61
Freedom Movement, ix, x, xiin1
"The Future of Race" (interview), 93

Garvey, Marcus, 58
Gates, Henry Louis, 93, 95–97, 100
Ghana, 77, 95
Gilroy, Paul, 16, 17
Gloster, Hugh Morris, 15, 16
Gold Coast, 78
Gordon, Lewis, 69

Great Depression, Black community and, 69

Hamer, Fannie Lou, 12
Harlem Renaissance, 54, 95
Harris, Abram, 94
Harris, Leonard, 52, 62
Harrison, Hubert, 47, 55–57, 61, 63
Hayes, Rutherford B., 49
Hayes-Tilden Act (1877), 83
Hayes/Tilden Compromise (1877), 49
HBCUs, xi
Hegel, 32, 35, 59
Hip Hop, 73
history, unfolding of, 59
"Homo Africanus Harlemi" (Harrison), 57
horizon, 7
Hose, Sam, 27
Howard University, 52, 94
Hughes, Langston, 62
human existence, value as problem of, 55–60

idealism, 63
imagination, 81
"Incident" (Cullen), 4, 18n6

Jackson, George, 99
jazz, 73, 91
Jefferson, Thomas, 28
The Jesse Jackson Phenomenon (Reed), vii, 99
Jesus and the Disinherited (Thurman), 3, 8, 86
Jim Crow, 77, 82, 83, 86
Jones, Claudia, 63
Jones, Leroi, 3
The Journal of Ethics, 52

King, Martin Luther, Jr., 3, 67, 72, 80, 83–85, 89, 97
King, Rodney, 10
Klan Act (1871), 49

knowledge: of blackness, 25; of experience, 23; experiential moment and, 24–25; purposes of, 61; of self, 6
Ku Klux Klan, 49

Ladd, George Trumball, 59
Lawson, Bill, 92
liberalism, 91, 92, 98, 100
life of the mind, 52
live, vii
lived experience, 43n2
Locke, Alain, 12, 47, 52–57, 62, 63, 86
The Luminous Darkness (Thurman), 79, 85
lynching, 40, 49
lynch mobs, 56

Malcolm X, 93
Mammonism, 52
mapping the movement, 9–15, 41–42
maps, 10
March on Washington, 80
Marx, Karl, 64
Marxism, 92, 95
Mays, Benjamin Elijah, 15, 16
McGary, Howard, 92
Mckay, Claude, 62
The Measure of Man (King, M. L., Jr.), 72
memory, 81
metaphysical thought, 34
metaphysics, 74
mind, 34
Mississippi Freedom Party, 12
modern era, ix–xi, 2, 15, 41, xiin1; after, 89; blackness meaning in, 15; experiential moment and, 24; freedom gaze and, 7–9; movement and, 9–15; *Plessy v. Ferguson* influence on, 32; social networks and, 90
Montgomery Bus Boycott, 92
Morehouse College, xi
Moses, Greg, 83

movement: toward freedom, 90; freedom as, 10; mapping, 9–15, 41–42; placement within, 13
music, 73
mysticism, 81

NAACP, 16, 93
nationalism, 18; racial exploitation and race prejudice and, 72
Native Son (Wright), 76
negritude, 21, 62, 74, 95, 100n4
The Negro's God (Mays), 15
Negro Voices in American Fiction (Gloster), 15
New Deal, 94
New Negro, 52, 54, 56, 62; freedom gazing and, 60–61
New Negro (journal), 56
Newton, Huey P., xi, 3, 48, 98, xiin1
Nicomachaean Ethics (Aristotle), 30
Nigger Heaven (Van Vechten), 57
Nkrumah, Kwame, 67, 72, 76–78, 85, 95

Omi, Michael, 83
oppression, 73; capitalism and, 98; physical violence and, 4; society and, 71
"Oration, Delivered in Corinthian Hall, Rochester, July 5, 1852" (Douglass), 11–12
otherness, 62, 67, 71, 75, 79
Outlaw, Lucious, 11

pain, 5
Pan African, 17
peace, 10–11, 13
perception, 81
perceptual frameworks: defining, 7; freedom gaze as, 7–9
personal autonomy, 92
phantasm, 43n6
phenomenal world, words and, 5–6
The Philadelphia Negro (Du Bois), 29
Philosophy Born of Struggle, xi

physical violence, oppression and, 4
Pinn, Anthony B., vii, 1
placement, within movement, 13
Plessy v. Ferguson, 8, 12, 32, 33, 44n21, 48, 49
political-class wars, 71, 72
pragmatic accommodationist thinkers, 62–63
pragmatism, 63, 94
prison resistance campaigns, 99
Prophesy Deliverance (West), 16
pseudoscience, 31, 33
Pullman Porters Union, 93

race: conceptions of, 44n22; culture and, 53, 55; political rights and, 83; as social construction, 52
race prejudice, 72
racial antagonism, 71–72
racial class divide, vii
racial discrimination, vii
racial exploitation, 72
Racial Formation in the United States (Omi and Winant), 83
racial hatred, 71
racial slavery, vii
racial vindicationism, 60
racism, 73
rebellion, 10–11, 13–14
recognition, 74
Reconstruction, 30
A Red Record (Wells), 39, 40
Reed, Adolph, Jr., vii, 18, 22, 96, 99, 100
reflective thinking, 19n14
reggae, 73
rejecting, 6
Republic of New Africa, 91
resistance, 99; rebellion and, 14
resisting, 6
revolution, 10–11, 14–15, 98
Revolutionary Suicide (Newton), 3
Revolution of Conscience (Moses), 83
rights: enforcement of, 28; liberalism and, 92; political, 83

right to life, 50
Robinson, Cedric, on Black Intelligentsia, 7
Rose, Charlie, 93

scalar quantities, of coordinating qualities, 10, 56
scholar activist, 35, 40, 61
SCLC, 93
segregation, alterity and, 79–82
self-definition, 16
self-realization, 26
sensory perception, cognition and, 23
separateness, 71, 75
Simmel, Georg, 41
slavery, 32, 76, 90; as death, 1; dehumanization and, 6–7; phenomena denoted by, 6
"Slavery, Paternalism, and Liberalism" (McGary), 92
socialism, 63
social movements, 92
social networks, 41, 47, 90
social transformation, 40, 48, 61; consciousness and, 25
society: oppression and, 71; political-class wars and, 71
"Society and Ideology" (Nkrumah), 78
socio-centric networks, 41
soul, 34
The Souls of Black Folk (Du Bois), 2, 3, 22, 30, 31, 36, 92; experiential moment and, 26–27; resisting and rejecting in, 6
Southern Horrors (Wells), 39, 40
spirit, 34
Sterling, James Hutchinson, 60
Stewart, Jeffrey C., 53
Stirrings in the Jug (Reed), 18
The Strange Career of Jim Crow (Woodward), 83
struggle: existential crisis and, 99; freedom and, 10, 48; rebellion and, 14

The Suppression of the African Slave Trade to the Americas (Du Bois), 29

temporospatial relationships, 10, 41–42
theoretical freedom, 39
thinking, 23
thought: about Black Experience, 11; metaphysical, 34; value as problem of, 52–55
Thurman, Howard, xi, 3, 8, 12, 48, 67, 72, 76, 86, xiin1; on distortion of humanness, 75; fragmentation and, 91, 92; freedom gazing and, 85; on segregation, 79–82
Toomer, Jean, 62
Transatlantic Slave Trade, 31
traveling, 81
Trotter, Monroe, 51

"The Uncomplete Argument" (Appiah), 44n22
UNIA. *See* United Negro Improvement Association
United Negro Improvement Association (UNIA), 58
Urban League, 16

value: as freedom, 47–52; as problem of human existence, 55–60; as problem of thought, 52–55
"Value and Imperatives" (Locke), 53
Van Vechten, Carl, 57
Vardaman, James K., 33
Vietnam War, 85
vigilantes, 56
violence: Black exploitation and, 40; oppression and, 4
voluntarism, 59

Walker, David, 35, 39
war: Black community and, 69; capitalism and, 71; political-class, 71–72
Washington, Booker T., 16, 96; accommodationism and, 33, 51–52,

63; Atlanta Compromise and, 33, 48–52; Du Bois and, 35; forgiveness and, 75–76, 89–90
Watts Riots, 92
Wells, Ida B., 39, 40, 42, 47, 63–64
West, Cornel, 16, 93, 95–97
Where Do We Go from Here (King, M. L., Jr.), 82, 84, 85, 89
Whewell, William, 51
Whitehead, Alfred North, 43n2, 81
Why, Lord? (Pinn), vii, 1
Why We Can't Wait (King, M. L., Jr.), 82
Winant, Howard, 83
Woodward, C. Vann, 83
words: phenomenal world and, 5–6; power of, 5
World War I, 85
World War II, 69
Wright, Richard, 75–76, 89–90

About the Author

Anthony Sean Neal is Beverly B. and Gordon W. Gulmon Humanities Professor at Mississippi State University. He is an associate professor of philosophy in the Department of Philosophy and Religion and faculty fellow in the Shackouls Honors College of Mississippi State University. He also has an affiliation with the Department of African American Studies. He is a 2019 inductee into the Morehouse College Collegium of Scholars and a fellow with the American Institute for Philosophical and Cultural Thought. Dr. Neal is visiting research fellow for the Warburg Institute in London and the 2022–2023 APA Edinburgh Fellow.

www.ingramcontent.com/pod-product-compliance
Lightning Source LLC
Chambersburg PA
CBHW020744020526
44115CB00030B/1023